Corporate
Finance

:: Author ::

Pareshkumar M. Thakor

PUBLISHED BY

Hemchandracharya International Publishing House
HQ. At & Po. Chaveli., Ta- Chansma,
Dist- Patan, North Gujarat, India, Asia.
www.iphouseindia.com

First Publication: 11th April, 2015

Copyright: Author

(c) **Pareshkumar M. Thakor**

ISBN:- 978-15-12121-85-8

Price: Rs.750/- INDIA
$ 15 OUTSIDE INDIA

PUBLISHED BY

**Hemchandracharya International Publishing House
HQ. At & Po. Chaveli., Ta- Chansma,
Dist- Patan, North Gujarat, India, Asia.
www.iphouseindia.com**

What is Corporate Finance ?

Corporate finance is one of the most important subjects in the financial domain. It is deep rooted in our daily lives. All of us work in big or small corporations. These corporations raise capital and then deploy this capital for productive purposes. **The financial calculations that go behind raising and successfully deploying capital is what forms the basis of corporate finance**. Here is a short introduction:

Separation of Ownership and Management

The basis of corporate finance is the separation of ownership and management. Now, the firm is not restricted by capital which needs to be provided by an individual owner only. The general public needs avenues for investing their excess savings. They are not content with putting all their money in risk free bank accounts. They wish to take a risk with some of their money. It is because of this reason that capital markets have emerged. They serve the dual need of providing corporations with access to source of financing while at the same time they provide the general public with a plethora of choices for investment.

Liaison between Firms and Capital Markets

The corporate finance domain is like a liaison between the firm and the capital markets. The purpose of the financial manager and other professionals in the corporate finance domain is twofold. Firstly, they need to ensure that the firm has adequate finances and that they are using the right sources of funds that have the minimum costs. Secondly, they have to ensure that the firm is putting the funds so raised to good use and generating maximum return for its owners. These two decisions are the basis of corporate finance and have been listed in greater detail below:

Financing Decision

As stated above the firm now has access to capital markets to fulfill its financing needs. However, the firm faces multiple choices when it comes to financing. The firm can firstly choose whether it wants to raise equity capital or debt capital. Even within the equity and debt capital the firm faces multiple choices. They can opt for a bank loan, corporate loans, public fixed deposits, debentures and amongst a wide variety of options to raise funds. With financial innovation and securitization, the range of instruments that the firm can use to raise capital has become very large. The job of a financial manager therefore is to ensure that the firm is well capitalized i.e. they have the right amount of capital and that the firm has the right capital structure i.e. they have the right mix of debt and equity and other financial instruments.

Investment Decision

Once the firm has gained access to capital, the financial manager faces the next big decision. This decision is to deploy the funds in a manner that it yields the maximum returns for its shareholders. For this decision, the firm must be aware of its cost of capital. Once they know their cost of capital, they can deploy their funds in a way that the returns that accrue are more than the cost of capital which the company has to pay. Finding such investments and deploying the funds successfully is the investing decision. It is also known as capital budgeting and is an integral part of corporate finance.

Capital budgeting has a theoretical assumption that the firm has access to unlimited financing as long as they have feasible projects. A variation of this decision is capital rationing. Here the assumption is that the firm has limited funds and must choose amongst competing projects even though all of them may be financially viable. The firm thus has to select only those projects that will provide the best return in the long term.

Financing and investing decisions are like two sides of the same coin. The firm must raise finances only when it has suitable avenues to deploy them. The domain of corporate finance has various tools and techniques which allow managers to evaluate financing and investing decisions. It is thus essential for the financial well being of a firm.

Nominal and Real Value of Money

The previous one was an introduction about the two basic decisions that corporate finance helps a corporation in making. Prima-facie, these two decisions may look pretty simple. After all everyone raises money in their daily lives and puts it to productive use. Simple accounting can tell us whether or not we should make those financing and investing decisions. So, why is there a need for a complicated subject called corporate finance to make these decisions? Well, it turns out there is a need? The need arises because of this concept of nominal and real value of money. This one will explain why corporate finance is required:

The Concept of Inflation

We are all intuitively aware of the concept of inflation. We know that money loses its value every year. The same amount of money will purchase less and less every year. Let's say that $100 is required to purchase a certain commodity of goods today. So if there is an inflation of 10%, the same goods will be available for a $110 next year.

Introduction to Nominal Value of Money

So, if we made an investment that was yielding 9% return this year, we would have a total of $109 next year from the $100 we had invested. In accounting terms we would have a profit of $9. This is because we are only considering the nominal values.

Nominal values do not consider the effect of inflation, opportunity cost of capital and such other forces which cause the value of money to decrease in a given time period.

The Problem with Nominal Values to Measure a Firm's Performance:

Nominal values present a distorted image of the firm's performance to its shareholders and this is to say the least. Consider the case we discussed above. Here, the firm has lost 1% purchasing power. This means they were better off consuming the $100 in year 1 and could have purchased more goods with it rather than investing it and consuming $109 a year later. Thus, if nominal values are considered, firms will end up eroding their capital by investing their money in projects that offer a rate of return that is below the firm's cost of capital.

Introduction to Real Value of Money

To offset this problem, specialists in corporate finance have come up with the concept of real value of money. The real value of money takes into account inflation, opportunity cost of capital and such other forces. Thus, firms that base their calculations on these inflation adjusted values make better financial decisions as compared to those that do not. The calculation for both real as well as nominal values is simple and can be done with the help of the following formula:

Real Value = Nominal Value / (1 + (i / 100))

i = The prevailing inflation rate in the market

Subjectivity in Real Value of Money:

It must be understood that the real and nominal values of money are subjective. This is because, they are determined using the inflation rate. There is no single measure of inflation. The government itself produces multiple estimates of inflation. Also, for the purpose of the company's calculation, these measures may not be good enough. So the company may create its own inflation index depending on which the real values are calculated. Thus, there is widespread subjectivity in this calculation. Different companies use different rates to convert nominal values to real values.

The biggest take-away from the concept of nominal and real values is that money in one time period is not directly comparable to money in another time period. It is for this reason we have to calculate present values, future values and the like. These calculations form the backbone of corporate finance.

Two Fundamental Rules of Corporate Finance

Corporate finance is based on two fundamental rules. All tools and techniques of corporate finance are mere ways and means of implementing these rules. These rules can be found at the beginning of any and every corporate finance text book. **One of these rules relates to the concept of return while the other relates to the concept of risk.** We have described both these rules in this one. They are as follows:

Rule # 1: Money today is worth more than money tomorrow

The fundamental rule of corporate finance is that the timing of cash flows is of paramount importance. Also, we want the timing of the cash flows to be as soon as possible. The sooner we get the cash, the better it is for our company. Every dollar that the company has in cash today is better than the same dollar in cash tomorrow because of the following reasons:

- **Inflation:** Inflation eats into the purchasing power of the company's funds constantly with the passage of time. Thus if the company had the same nominal amount of money today or a year from now, they would be able to purchase more goods and services with the money that they have today as compared to the same amount of money a year later. Thus, to offset the effect of inflation, companies must conduct their business in a manner that they ensure that cash is received as soon as possible.

- **Opportunity Cost:** Also, every dollar that the company is not receiving has an opportunity cost of capital. Let's say the company's debtors owe it $100 and they pay $100 the next year. The nominal value of the money that they have paid is $100 however the real value is less. This is because had the debtors paid immediately, the company would have cash immediately on hand. They could then invest this cash in risk free securities and could have earned a year's interest on the same. By accepting the same $100 a year later, the company has in effect loaned out $100 to its debtors and that too interest free!

Rule # 2: Risk free money is worth more than risky money

Corporate finance involves exchanging between present and future streams of cash flows. Companies may come across different projects which offer different future cash flows. However, it is important to realize that all cash flows are not equally likely to materialize in the future. Some cash flows may be almost certain like investing in treasury bonds while others may be highly uncertain like projected returns from stock market investments. Hence, the second rule states that the company must adjust each of these cash flows for their risk before making any comparisons and selections. The following factors must be considered:

- **Return of Capital:** Some projects are extremely risky. Here, the company is concerned about whether or not the money they are investing will be recovered. A higher rate of return must be demanded from such projects to offset the likelihood of losing their entire capital that the investors face.
- **Return on Capital:** In other cases the cash flow may be a little less uncertain. In these cases, companies must consider the low risk before making their decision.

The bottom line is that before making a choice, all projects have to be made comparable. This is done by adjusting for cash flow that will be received in different time periods as well as adjusting for the different amounts of risks that are involved in different projects.

Present Value and Future Value of Money

Value of Money Depends Upon Time

In the previous One we learned about the concept of nominal and real values of money. We realized that money today is more valuable than the same sum received at a future date because there is no risk involved in obtaining it and also the real value of money is not expected to decrease by the time we receive it.

The simple implication of this is that we cannot compare the dollars we have on hand today to the dollars that we have been promised at a future date. In corporate finance, we call the value of money that we have on hand today the present value and the value of amount of money that we will receive at a future date the future value of money.

In corporate finance, we may often come across complex schedules of payments and receipts. Sometimes cash may have to be paid today while sometimes we may have to pay it at a later date. Similarly the receipts may be today or at a later date. Hence, to calculate, we must first convert all the values to present values. This One will explain how to do so with the help of an example:

Calculating Future Values

Let's understand the future values calculation with the help of an example. Let's say that we have $1000 today and we have calculated that our cost of capital is 10%. This 10% reflects both the expectation of inflation i.e. fall in the real value of money as well as the risk involved in this investment. Let's consider that we have to invest this money for a period of 3 years.

The formula for calculating the future values is as follows:

Future Value = Present Value $(1 + (\text{cost of capital} / 100)^{\text{number of years}}$

i.e. Future Value = $ $1000(1.10)^3$

i.e. Future Value = $ 1331

This means that the equivalent sum of money that we should expect in 3 years, given our cost of capital is $1331. This means that we should accept proposals where future value is more than $1331, reject proposals where future value is less than $1331 and be indifferent towards proposals where future value is equal to $1331.

From henceforth, we will refer to this by stating that the future value of $1000, at our given cost of capital, for a period of 3 years is $1331. Also, it must be noted that future values are nominal in nature.

Present Values

Present values are the exact opposite of future values. During future values we were compounding a present value at a given rate to reach a future value. But in present value calculations, we will discount the future values, which are nominal in nature, at the given cost of capital for the given period to reach the present value. Let's look at it with the help of an example.

Now, we have a proposal that offers to pay us $1000, 3 years from hence. Our given cost of capital is 10%.

The formula for calculating the present values is as follows:

Present Value = Future Value / (1 + (cost of capital / 100)$^{\text{number of years}}$

i.e. Present Value = $1000 / (1.10)^3$

i.e. Present Value = $ 751.31

This means that the equivalent sum of money that we should expect today, given our cost of capital is $751.31. This means that we should accept proposals where present value is more than $751.31, reject proposals where present value is less than $751.31 and be indifferent towards proposals where future value is equal to $751.31.

When the term present value is used, finance professionals are referring to the discounted present day values which are equivalent to nominal future values.

The concept of present values and future values form the basis of corporate finance. Hence, it is essential that any student be well versed with these concepts. Variations of these concepts will be regularly used throughout the corporate finance course and hence due attention must be paid to mastering this concept before moving forward.

Net Present Value Calculations

The net present value (NPV) is the most important concept in corporate finance. It is on the basis of this concept that investment decisions are made or not made. It is on the basis of this concept that stocks and bonds are valued. Thus, it is an absolute imperative for any student of corporate finance to be thoroughly well versed with this concept. One needs to have a fair understanding of future and present value calculations to understand the net present value concept. The NPV is best understood with the help of a cash flow timeline. This One will use the same to explain it:

The Cash Flow Timeline:

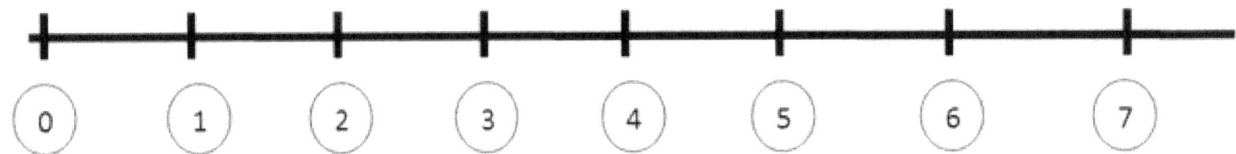

The cash flow timeline is a representation of the periods when cash is expected to be paid or received during the project. Point Zero, represents today. Hence all the amounts listed in point Zero are present values. We do not have to adjust them by compounding or discounting for the net present value calculations.

The values listed under point 1 are the amounts that will be received or paid at the end of period one. The values listed under period 2 are the amounts that will be received or paid at the end of period 2, so on and so forth.

Future Values Occur In Different Periods

When we compare two numbers, we must ensure that that are of similar nature. Hence, when comparing cash flows we must ensure that all of them are either present values or future values belonging to the same future period. Comparing a present value to a future value or comparing a future value in period 1 to a future value in period 2 is like comparing apples to oranges.

Since future values all occur in different periods, we cannot compare them with each other. The only way to add or subtract these values is if we bring them all back to day zero i.e. convert every future value to their equivalent present values.

Present Values Occur at the Same Time i.e. Day Zero

Since present values depict the value of money on day zero i.e. in the same period, it would be correct for us to add, subtract or perform any other mathematical operation on this number. The key point to understand is that all values involved in the calculation must be present values.

NPV Calculation Example

Let's consider the following schedule of cash outflows and inflows:

Period 0: $10,000 Cash Outflow

Period 1: $5,000 Inflow

Period 2: $4,000 Inflow

Period 3: $3,500 Inflow

Period 4: $3,000 Inflow

Cost of Capital is 10%.

The question is whether it is financially wise to invest $10,000 today and receive 4 installments of $5000, $4000, $3500 and $3000 if our cost of capital is 10%.

Solution:

Outflow: $10,000

Present Value of Inflows: PV (Inflow in Year 1) + PV (Inflow in Year 2) + PV (Inflow in Year 3) + PV (Inflow in Year 4)

$= (\$5,000/1.1)^1 + (\$4,000/1.1)^2 + (\$3,500/1.1)^3 + (\$3,000/1.1)^4$

$= \$4,545.46 + \$3,305.79 + \$2,629.60 + \$2,049.04$

$= \$12,529.89$

Net Present Value = Present Value of Inflows − Present Value of Outflows

$= \$12,529 - \$10,000$

$= \$2,529$

Net Present Value Rule

The net present value rule states that if the NPV of the proposal is greater than 0, it must be accepted. For less than and equal to zero the proposals must be rejected. In this case, the NPV is $2529. Hence, this proposal is financially sound given the cost of capital of the firm. It would be in their best interest to accept this proposal.

Compounding Intervals and Interest Rate

Theoretically there are two types of interest rates, simple and compounding. However, in finance the word interest usually refers to compound interest. Simple interest almost never factors in financial calculations. In all calculations related to present values and future values, compound interest is used. However, **as a student of corporate finance, it is essential to know the difference that compounding intervals have on the effective interest rate that is paid on the investment**. This One explains the same:

Simple Interest vs. Compound Interest

We are all aware of the difference between simple and compound interest. However, just to reiterate, the principal amount never changes in a simple interest calculation. So if $100 are lent for 3 years at 10% simple interest, the interest paid in each of the 3 years would be $10.

But if $100 were lent at 10% for 3 years and compounding happens annually, the interest payments would be $10, $11 and

$13.1 for years 1,2 and 3 respectively. This is because at the end of each period the accrued interest gets added to the principal and therefore the interest in the next period is a little bit more.

Annual vs. Semi-Annual Compounding

In case of compound interest 10% compounded annually and 10% compounded semi-annually i.e. twice a year do not means the same thing. Let's understand this with the help of an example:

Annual Compounding: $100 @10%, Interest = $10

Semi-Annual Compounding: $100 @10%, Interest $5 after 6 months and %5.25 after another 6 months. Hence the total interest would be $10.25 as opposed to $10 on an annual basis.

Rates Increase As Compounding Intervals Grow Smaller:

As we can see from the above example that semi-annual rates give more interest than the annual rates. We can extend this logic further and say that monthly rates will provide more interest as compared to semi-annual rates and weekly rates will provide more interest than monthly rates.

As a thumb rule, we can say that the smaller the compounding intervals, the higher the interest rates will be. As far as investments are concerned, most rates are compounded annually or semi-annually. Smaller compounding frequencies are not used. In common usage, only in the case of credit cards are the rates expressed as monthly compounding interest rates.

Continuous Compounding

Until now, we have considered discrete intervals at which interest was being paid. We could bring the intervals down to hours, minutes or even seconds and yet they will be discrete. Theoretically it is possible that interest be paid continuously over a given period of time. This is not possible in reality. However, continuously compounded interest rates provide some ease in mathematical calculations. It is for this reason that they are often used in finance. Compounded interest rates can be converted into continuously compounded interest rates by multiplying them with — e^{rt}

Where:

$e = 2.718$

r = annually compounded rate of interest

t = number of time periods

Opportunity Cost of Capital

Opportunity cost of a capital is a term unique to economics and finance. It is unique in the sense that you will not find mention of opportunity cost of capital in the accounting books. It is not an explicit cost which is paid out of the pocket. Hence, there is no mention of this cost in the accounting records. Rather, it is an implicit cost which results out of our investment decisions. This One will explain about opportunity cost of capital and how it must be used while making financial decisions:

Alternate Uses of Money

Opportunity cost of capital represents alternate uses of money. Let's say, if I have a $1000 to invest and I decide to invest the money in the stock market, I am committing my resources. By investing $1000 in the stock market, I will now not be able to use the same $1000 for any other purposes now. I must therefore ensure that I am committing my resources to the best possible project. Let's say, I have a choice between real estate and stock market investment, when I choose the stock market investment, I make it my best possible choice. Opportunity cost of capital tells us what we are foregoing to choose that best possible alternative. Opportunity cost of capital is therefore the value of the second best alternative.

Alternate Projects Must Share Similar Risk Profile

However, **we must ensure that we compare opportunity costs of capital across similar projects**. This will ensure that we do not see a biased picture and end up choosing the wrong projects. Consider a comparison between a stock market investment and government bonds. Usually, stock markets will offer more return compared to government bonds. So, using government bonds as the opportunity cost will always make them look good. But stock market investments and government bond investments have very different risk profiles. One guarantees a fixed rate of return whereas there are no guarantees in the other. Hence, using one as the opportunity cost of capital for another will provide a skewed picture and the risky alternative will always be chosen. Hence, only projects with similar risk must be used for opportunity cost of capital calculation. This makes these calculations very subjective and open to debate.

Alternate Uses Represent Implicit Costs

The investment decision is all about prioritizing. It is about choosing the best possible alternative. So, if we have 2 alternatives, one which offers a $100 return potential whereas another which offers an $80 return potential, then by choosing one alternative we are alternatively foregoing the other one. So, if we choose to get a $100 return, we are foregoing the $80 return. Corporate finance captures this implicit tradeoff in the expected rate of return number.

How Opportunity Cost Helps in Decision Making ?

Opportunity cost helps in choosing the right project when faced with a variety of alternatives. Here is how the decision is affected:

- **Higher Opportunity Cost Lowers NPV:** A higher opportunity cost implies a bigger discount rate. A bigger discount rate means that the future values are worth considerably less today. This creates a situation where the

NPV is lowered. A high opportunity cost of capital raises the bar for all other projects as well.

- **Only the Best Investment Has Positive NPV:** Also, we need to understand that in a given set of 2-3 investment proposals, only the best proposal will have a positive NPV. This is because the best proposal will be the opportunity cost of capital for the other projects. Since the opportunity cost of capital will be higher than the cash flows that the project has to offer, the NPV of such a project will be negative. One just needs to be careful about the risk profile of different projects to ensure an "apples to apples" comparison.

Valuing Cash Flows in Different Periods

Cash flows vary from project to project. In some cases cash flows will occur evenly over time. There might be payments of similar amounts that will be spread out over a time period at regular intervals. On the other hand, there might be payments which are irregular and have no pattern whatsoever. The challenge in corporate finance is to value these different streams of cash flows. Here is how this is done:

Present Value of a Stream of Cash Flows

The present value of a stream of cash flows can be expressed as a lump sum amount. This can be done only after all the expected future receipts are converted to their present day values. The sum of these values is then equal to the value of the expected stream of cash flows. This is exactly how the value of a future stream of payments is derived.

Nature of Cash Flows

The calculation of the present value of the future stream of money depends upon the nature of the cash flows. If the cash flows are spread out in an even pattern, shortcuts like annuities and perpetuities can be used and the value of large streams can also be calculated very easily. However, if the cash flows are uneven, individual payments have to be discounted to their present value and then all those payments need to be added up.

Inflation Forecasts May Change Over Time

Now, there are many investments that go on for a period of 10 years, 15 years and so on. The inflation forecast does not remain the same over such an extended period of time. In fact historically, the inflation will change every time there is a change in the business cycle. Hence, for investments over a long period of time, multiple inflation forecasts may be required where different rates are used in different years.

Uncertainty Increases with Time

Moreover, in projects where cash flow goes on for multiple years, the uncertainty also increases with increased time. It is a fundamental rule in corporate finance that the farther the expected payments are, the more uncertain they are. This is because over an extended period there might be political, economic or social changes that might affect the cash flows. Hence different rates may be used to discount the cash flows in different years to get a more accurate picture.

Multiple Discount Rates

Analysts almost always use multiple discount rates to represent the different uncertainties that cash flows in different years have inherent in them. Moreover, the value of the future cash flows is highly sensitive to discount rates. Hence, small changes in the discount rate can bring about big changes in valuation. This, coupled with the fact that discount rates are very difficult to predict in advance makes investing an art rather than a science.

What is Perpetuity ? - Definition and Concept

Perpetuity is a very important concept in corporate finance. The concept of perpetuity makes it possible to value stocks, real estate and many other investment opportunities. The valuation of perpetuities is theoretically very simple. The concept of perpetuity as well as the formula required for its calculation has been explained in this One:

Stream of Cash Flows that Never Terminates

In corporate finance, we try to compare the value of different streams of cash flows. Sometimes, we exchange a lump sum value for a finite stream of future payments. However, in case of perpetuity, the payments will never cease. A perpetuity is basically a stream of cash flows that never terminates. This means that if we purchase a perpetuity right now after paying a certain lump sum, we should expect repayments that last till the end of time.

Examples of Perpetuities

Although, valuing a perpetuity may not seem intuitive in the first place, it is required. There are many forms of investments that mimic the features of a perpetuity.

Consider the example of common stocks. Common stocks are basically an investment in the operations of a company. Theoretically the company has an infinite life. Therefore the shareholder is entitled to an infinite stream of future dividends for paying the stock price now. It is for this reason that common stocks are valued as a perpetuity.

Similarly consider the example of real estate. Once the purchase price of real estate has been paid, the owner is entitled to receive an infinite stream of rental payments. Thus real estate is also valued as a perpetuity.

Many universities have endowment funds that pay scholarships to students. They have been doing so for centuries and plan to continue to do so forever. These funds were invested in a perpetuity by a philanthropist many years ago. Now it continues to make payments till the end of time!

Why Perpetuities Have a Finite Value ?

The most counter-intuitive part of perpetuity is the fact that it has a finite value. The question that comes to everybody's mind is that how can a series of infinite cash flows have a finite valuation. The answer is because the real value of future cash flows keeps on falling. The present values are high in the early years. However, the payment amount is fixed under a perpetuity. Therefore in the later years as and when inflation keeps on increasing, the real value of the payments are continuously decreasing. It is because of this that the cash flows in the very distant future will have a near zero valuation although it will never exactly be zero. Hence using the formula for sum of an infinite series, the value of a perpetuity can be calculated.

Formula for Valuing Perpetuities

The formula for valuing perpetuities is very simple and straightforward. It is as follows:

$$PV = C / R$$

Where:

PV is the present value of perpetuity

C is the amount of cash flow received every period

R is the required rate of return

Growing Perpetuity

We have seen that a perpetuity represents an infinite stream of future cash flows. However, we have also seen that as time passes the value of these cash flows constantly diminishes. $100 may be able to buy us quite a few goods today, but in 50 years time $100 will not be nearly as valuable as it is today. It is for this reason that receiving infinite payments is not enough. The payments must also keep growing at a certain rate. This will ensure that they are not considerable behind inflation. This is the idea behind a growing perpetuity. The same has been explained in detail in this One:

Growing Infinite Payments

As already stated, a **growing perpetuity involves payments that do not remain fixed**. Instead these payments keep on growing at the same constant rate of growth. So, if the rate of growth of the payments is 7%, each payment will be 7% more than the payment received before it.

Present Value of a Growing Perpetuity

The present value of a growing perpetuity can be derived from a complex mathematical calculation. This is because a growing perpetuity is also an infinite series which has a finite sum. For our purposes, we can just remember the formula required for our calculation.

Present Value (Growing Perpetuity) = D / (R - G)

Where:

D = Expected cash flow in period 1

R = Expected rate of return

G = Rate of growth of perpetuity payments

However, we need to understand that for this formula to hold true, G must always be greater than R. If G is less than R or equal to R, the formula does not hold true. This is because, the stream of payments will cease to be an infinitely decreasing series of numbers that have a finite sum.

Examples:

Growing perpetuities are found in a variety of places in our daily lives. Some of them have been mentioned below:

- **College endowment funds** need to be growing perpetuities. This is because with the passage of time, tuition and other expenses will become more and more expensive. Hence the college endowment funds must keep growing to meet the scholarship demands represented by growing expenses.

- **Stock valuations** always assume a growing perpetuity for their terminal value calculation. Without the concept of a growing perpetuity it would be impossible to value a stock.

- **Loss of Real Value of Money:** Since the formula assumes that the growth rate of the perpetuity will always be less than the required rate of return, it is implying a loss scenario. This is because, no matter what the case, the growth rate can, by definition, never be more than the required rate of return.

The growing perpetuity, thus assumes that we will lose a small amount of the real value of money every year. Just like the perpetuity, a growing perpetuity can only be summed up because the series is infinitely decreasing. The growing perpetuity assumes that we will lose the real value of money at a slower rate as compared to an ordinary perpetuity.

What is Annuity ? - Meaning and Concept

An annuity, just like a perpetuity, is a shortcut used while making present value calculations. Unlike the perpetuity, which is very difficult to find in real life, we find examples of annuity all around us. The monthly mortgage payments we make, the car loan or student loan that we pay off are all annuities. **Annuities play a very important role in corporate finance. They form the basis for valuation of bonds and other financial instruments**. This One provides more information about the concept of an annuity:

Finite Stream: The first and foremost difference between an annuity and a perpetuity is the fact that an annuity has a finite life. Unlike perpetuities, annuities do not go on forever. It is for this reason that we they are conceptually more intuitive and easy to understand.

Equal Amounts: A stream of payments can be called an annuity, if and only if, all the payments in that stream of future cash flows is of equal amounts. For instance, if the future cash flows for 4 consecutive years from now are $100 in each year, then this stream is called an annuity. On the other hand, if the future cash flows for the next 3 years are $100 and the 4th year is $110, then this stream of cash flows cannot be called an annuity. (It is an annuity if you consider years 1 to 3)

Equal Time Lag: Every payment in the stream of cash flows should be equally spaced. This means that if payments are being made on a monthly basis, all payments should be made on a monthly basis. If the time lag when payments are made is changing, then the cash flow schedule cannot be classified as an annuity. This is because the annuity formula assumes that the cash flows are evenly spaced out.

Same Interest Rate: A stream of cash flows can be called an annuity, if the interest rate being charged throughout the period is same. For instance, if the rate of interest across the entire duration of a 10 year loan is 10%, then the stream of payments can be classified as an annuity. On the other hand, if the rate of interest keeps varying from year to year, then it cannot be valued as an annuity because the annuity calculation formula assumes the same interest rate.

Amortization Concept: The payments in an annuity represent amortization of a lump sum amount. This means that although the amount paid in installments is constant, its internal components are changing.

Let's understand this, with the help of an example. Let's say that there is a $100 payment per month for the next 5 years. Now, the $100 amount will remain constant for the next 5 years, however the internal components will change. The first payment may represent an $80 interest charge and $20 repayment of principal while the last payment may only represent $10 interest and $90 repayment of principal. This is called amortization.

The first few payments in an annuity have very high interest components. With the passage of time, the interest component becomes smaller and smaller and repayment of principal amounts becomes larger and larger.

Ordinary Annuity vs. Annuity Due

Annuities can be divided into two types based on the exact time when the payments occur in a given period. The payments could either occur at the beginning of every period or the payments could occur at the end of every period. For instance when you take a house on rent, the rent is usually paid in advance whereas when your mortgage payments are usually made at the end of every period. So **the payments made at the end of every period are called ordinary annuity**. This is because ordinary annuity is the usual state of affairs. Usually all annuities are paid at the end of the period.

Alternatively, **when annuity payments are made in advance, we call them annuity due**. The difference in the formula to calculate the two different types of annuities is very small. Also, the difference in amounts is not expected to be large either. However, to be precise, a student of finance must know the difference between ordinary annuity and annuity due and know when to use the formulas.

One Extra Period

As we seen that ordinary annuity payments are made at the end of each period whereas the payments for annuity due are made at the beginning of each period. Hence, the difference between ordinary annuity and annuity due is one extra period. Thus, an adjustment needs to be made for this one extra period while calculating both the present value and future value of an annuity due.

Future Value of an Annuity Due: Let's say that we want to calculate the future value of an annuity which pays $100 for 5 years and the payments begin at the beginning of the first period. The rate of interest is 10%

If we used the regular annuity formula or table, we would be given the future value of the above case as $610.51. However, this is the value if the payments were made at the end of each period. To convert them into annuity due we need to account for the one extra period. So we further multiply the answer by (1+i). In our case, since the interest rate is 10% per annum, we multiply it by 1.1. So the future value of the same example would be $610.51*(1.1). In this case the answer is $671.56

Calculating the present value of annuity due is a simple 2 step procedure:

- First, you calculate the future value as a regular annuity
- Secondly, you compound the future value, so derived, for an additional period

Present Value of an Annuity Due: Let's say that you were to receive 5 annual payments of $100 each for the next 5 years beginning at beginning of each period and your required rate of return is 10% per annum.

If we used the regular annuity formula or table, we would be given the present value of the above case as $379.08. However, this is the value if the payments were made at the end of each period. To convert them into annuity due we need to account for the one extra period. So we further divide the answer by (1+i). In our case, since the interest rate is 10% per annum, we divide it by 1.1. So the present value of the same example would be $379.08/(1.1). In this case the answer is $344.6.

Calculating the present value of annuity due is a simple 2 step procedure:

- First, you calculate the present value as a regular annuity

- Secondly, you discount the present value for an additional period

Please note the difference. While calculating future values, we compounded the result for an extra period i.e. we multiplied. On the other hand, while computing present values, we discounted for one extra period i.e. we divided the result.

The concept of annuity due will be hidden in the question i.e. it will not be explicitly stated. Hence, one must pay attention to when the payments are being made to determine whether it is an ordinary annuity or an annuity due.

Different Types of Annuity Calculations

In the One on present value, we learnt that the value of a dollar today is not the same as it will be 10 years from now. Then, we came across annuities which are a powerful mechanism that ensure that the nominal value of the payments remain the same throughout the years whereas its internal components i.e. interest and principal keep on changing. Annuities, therefore give a very useful way to work with a schedule of payments. **There are various types of payment schedules possible while working with an annuity. Here are some of the important types:**

Lump Sum to Annuity Payments

Annuities can convert a lump sum payment today into a series of future cash flows which will have the exact same value as of today. This is useful in business because usually the outlays required have to be done immediately in a lump sum whereas the benefits arrive at a later date and they arrive in installments. Annuities therefore enable us to draw a comparison between these values and decide if they are beneficial to us.

Example: Assuming a 12% rate of return for the next 5 years, an annual payment of $27.74 has the same present value as a $100 payment today. So we can choose between making a $100 payment upfront or choose a 5 year annuity of $27.74

Annuity Payments to Lump Sum

The reverse of the above calculation is also true. Annuities help us to take a series of future equal payments that will be made at equal periodic intervals and come up with a lump sum present value that is equal to those payments. This too is very useful. Let's say that you are scheduled to make mortgage payments for the next 5 years. But instead you choose to pay upfront and close the loan. What is the amount that you should pay to the lender? Annuity calculations will help us come up with that amount.

Example: Assuming a 14% interest rate for the next 5 years and an annual payment of $100, the present value of this stream of payments is $343.31

Partial Lump Sum

Now, in the above cases we were converting lump sums into equal payments or equal annuity payments into lump sums. Annuity calculations can be used to arrive at the calculation of the two as well. The payment maybe partially made in equal installments and partially paid in a lump sum. For instance, if you owed the bank $500, you could pay $200 upfront and convert the balance into an annuity.

Annuity calculations allow you to convert any lump sum or stream of cash flows into any other lump sum or stream of cash flows or a combination of both. These calculations form the backbone of finance and it is difficult to imagine the financial world without them.

What is Bond Valuation and How is it Calculated ?

One of the Most Important Uses of Discounting

The present value of a bond is the sum of all the future cash flows that can be derived from it. In this sense, the valuation of bonds really becomes simple, isn't it? All we need to do is find out the future stream of payments that are due on the bond and then find out their present value and we call find out what the valuation of that bond is. Well, this may be theoretically this simple.

However, in practical life estimating the parameters like discount rate which go into the calculation can be very difficult. Also, using different discount rates can cause us to come up with very different valuations. So, bond valuation really is a game about guessing what the future discount rate will be.

Now, let's have a look at a theoretical example of bond valuation. Here is a step by step procedure of how the calculation must be done:

Two Components

The calculation of the present value of the bond is done in two components. They are as follows:

- **Annuity:** Bonds have a series of coupon payments that are due. Coupon payments are interest payments that are made periodically. Usually the frequency of paying interest is semi-annual. Corporations all over the world pay interest twice a year because it is a bond market convention. Also, it must be understood that bonds can have 2 values. The face value is the original issue value of the bond whereas the market value is its current market price. So, if the interest payments are not directly given, we need to compute them using the face value. Remember that interest payments are always computed using face value and not market value!

  Hence, the annual interest rate needs to be converted into a semi-annual rate or whatever rate is appropriate. Then, it must be plugged into the annuity formula along with the other details to derive the present value of the coupon payments that are due.

- **Lump sum:** Bonds usually pay interest throughout their lives. However, they pay back the principal at the end of their lives. The principal therefore is a lump sum payment that may have to be discounted many years into the future. Now, even though this payment is not being received twice a year, we will still consider the semi-annual interest rates to find out the present value of the lump sum payment.

The final step is to add the present value of the annuity as well as of the lump sum payment. This adds the present values of the interest payments as well as the principal payments. Hence, we get the present value of the bond.

Example:

Let's find the present value of a bond whose face value is $100. Interest rate is 12% on an annual basis. The bond will make semi-annual interest payments for 10 years after which the principal has to be repaid and the bond expires.

Present Value of Interest Payments

Number of periods = 20 periods (10 years, however the payment is semi-annual)

Discount Rate = 6% per period (Since we have doubled the number of periods, we need to cut the discount rate into half)

Payment: $6 per period (6% * face value of $100)

Therefore, present value of the annuity equals $68.82. This is the present value of the interest payments due.

Present Value of Principal Due

The principal that needs to be repaid is $100. It needs to be repaid after 20 periods and the discount rate we are considering is 6% per period. The present value of the principal therefore is $31.18

To find the present value of the bond we need to add $68.82 + $31.18. In this case, this adds up to $100. Therefore the present value of the bond is $100.

It must, however be noted that in real life bond values swing based on the expectation of what the future discount rate will be like. It is not really the current discount rate which determines the bond value!

Bond Market Conventions

While calculating present values of bonds, one may observe that some of the information required to compute the present value is actually missing from the question. However, this is not an error. One needs to understand that the examiner is in a way testing your knowledge of how the bond market works. In the bond market, some of the information is considered to be implied i.e. it is not explicitly communicated. This is called the bond market convention. Here is a list of some of the commonly used conventions in the bond market:

Face Value Convention: If the face value of the bond is explicitly given, then the explicit face value must be used. However, if the face value is not explicitly given then the implied value is either $100 or $1000. Students can choose any of these values as the face values. They may state this in their assumptions for deriving the solution. But that too may not be required because bond market convention dictates that these values must be considered the face value in the absence of appropriate data.

Interest Rates Are Semi-Annual: Once again, a student needs to check if the frequency of the interest rates has been explicitly mentioned. In case it is, then we must use the interest rates that correspond to the frequency. However, in case they are not given, we need to use semi-annual interest rates. Most bond markets across the world pay interest twice a year. Hence, it is a reasonable assumption to make. Changing the annual interest rate into a semi-annual one has a huge change on the present value of the bond.

Day Count Conventions: Day count conventions specify the number of days that a year contains according to the bond market. The number of days in a year is important to the calculation of the interest that has been accrued on the bond. The day count convention, however, is not uniform in bond markets across the world. Each market has its own convention and the trader must be aware of the type of convention being used in the specific market that they are concerned about. However, day count conventions can be broadly classified into 3 categories:

- The year is assumed to be composed of 360 days
- The year is assumed to be composed of 365 days
- The year is assumed to be composed of the actual number of days i.e. 365 or 366 in a leap year

Interest Payments: Another convention that we need to discuss about is when the interest payment actually gets made. Now, once again this depends on the specific bond that is being considered. However, there are terms like EOM which denote that interest will be paid at the end of every month. Any student of bond valuation must be well versed with these terms as well as the implications that using these terms has on the valuation of the bond.

This list of conventions is obviously not comprehensive. There are many more conventions that may apply to all the markets across the globe or maybe specific to a given market. However, this One was meant to indicate that sometimes there might be information implied in the question even though one does not explicitly see the information mentioned.

How Changes in Interest Rates Affect Bonds ?

Interest rates are one of the most important factors while determining the bond value. All other factors like payments, number of periods etc are standard i.e. the numbers supplied to us are the numbers that have to be used in the formula for calculating present value. However, this is not the case with interest rates. Interest rates are subjective.

The number used in the formula depends upon the intuition and judgment of the investor. Since different investors use different interest rates while making their calculation, they arrive at different fair values for the same bond. Hence, there is difference of opinion. Some people may find the bond undervalued while some may find it overvalued. This is why trade takes place.

However, we need to be aware as to how different assumptions about the interest rates affect the value of the bond. Let's have a look at the same in this One:

Inverse Relation

Interest rates have an inverse relation with bonds and all fixed income securities in general. This simply means that an interest rate fall will lead to a price increase in the value of a bond whereas a rise in interest rate will lead to a fall in the market value of the bond. Theoretically the rise and fall happens after the news of the interest rate change has become known to the public at large i.e. it is a fact. However, in reality the market prices in expected changes in the interest rates. So by the time, the interest rates are announced, the value is already priced in and the fall or rise is relatively smaller. The important point is that the market works on opinions or future expectations and not on the basis of facts.

Example:

Let's consider the example of a bond which has a face value of $1000. It has a coupon rate of 10% per annum and is expected to pay semi-annual coupons for the next 4 years. So we need to see 3 possibilities:

1. **When Market Interest Rates are the Same as the Coupon Value ?:** When the interest rates are at 10%, the market value of this bond is $1000 as per the discounted cash flow valuation model for bond prices

2. **When Market Interest Rates are Greater than the Coupon Value?:** When the interest rates are at 12%, the market value of this bond is $900.65 as per the discounted cash flow valuation model for bond prices. Note as the interest rates went up from 10% to 12%, the value of the bond fell from $1000 to $900.

3. **When Market Interest Rates are Less than the Coupon Value?:** When the interest rates are at 8%, the market value of this bond is $1114.93 as per the discounted cash flow valuation model for bond prices. Note as the interest rates went up from 10% to 8%, the value of the bond fell from $1000 to $1114.93.

Logic behind Inverse Relation

The logic behind the inverse relation is really simple too. In case of fixed income securities we have locked in the nominal value of the money that we will receive. So the coupon payments are going to be the same, no matter what the interest rate is. This is because the coupon payments are fixed anyways.

But it is the real value of money which changes. So when interest rates go up, investors have the opportunity to invest their money in other bonds which currently have a higher yield. Our bond would therefore be overpriced in real terms. The value of the bond will therefore have to fall till it is fairly valued with other bonds in terms of its real value.

Common Stock Valuation: The Two Approaches

Ever since the inception of corporation as a separate legal entity, the common stock has become one of the most important financial instruments in the world today. When people commonly refer to the "market", they are usually referring to the stock market. For laymen, investing is synonymous with stocks. Yet the average person does not know much about how stocks ought to be valued. This One will explain how common people value stock prices and how it differs from the theoretical model:

- **The Theoretical Model**

  Theories state that shares actually represent fractional ownership. Therefore if you own 1% shares in a company, the value of the shares should be 1% of the expected value of the company. Now, when we say expected value, we must understand that value will only accrue in the future as and when the company conducts business over time. At the present moment, there are expectations and opinions about the future value. We need to discount these hypothetical future values at the correct discount rate to arrive at the future valuation of the company. Once, this future valuation is derived it, we can extrapolate the value of the share from it.

For instance, if the value of the entire company turns out to be $100, then the value of 1% of its stock should be $1. This is the scientific basis for arriving at a share price valuation. The advantage is that this method is much more objective than the other methods. Using this method, one can know what they think is the fair worth of a company. Then they can decide whether or not the current market price presents an undervalued opportunity to buy! This is called the discounted cash flow (DCF) method and henceforth we will be discussing this method.

- **The Behavioral Model**

The theoretical model is great theoretically. However, many a times it may not be practiced in real life. The reason behind this is simple. DCF models require a lot of information. Then the assume that the investor is skilled enough to make sense of all this information, organize it and arrive at the correct price. But, that's not what happens.

Usually people look at the past record of the stock, the record of how the peers of the company are performing etc. They try to have a very slight idea about how the future developments in the industry are expected to play out and how any given company stands to gain or lose from it. Based, on this very rough heuristic, they decide whether or not they want to buy a share.

The problem with this approach is that it promotes bubbles. Since there is no objective valuation, the share that is already rising in price will appear attractive and more people will want to buy it taking the price even further. Same is the case with declining prices too!

So this method is not really grounded in strong reality. Assuming the future will play out like the past is not a reasonable assumption. Hence, the DCF method is always preferred to any guessing game. The rest of the One will discuss about the theoretically correct DCF approach to stock valuation.

Stock Valuation - The Discounted Cash Flow Approach in Detail

In the past One we have seen how Discounted Cash Flow (DCF) is the most appropriate method of stock valuation because it is rational and objective. Now, it is time we have a look at the details of this model.

Present Value of Expected Future Cash Flows

The basic of this model seems to be simple. Any company is only worth as much as it will generate in cash flows over its lifetime. So, we need to estimate the lifetime of the company, we need to estimate the cash that the company is expected to turn in during this lifetime. Then we should discount the cash flows reflecting the risk and time duration. Adding up those cash flows should give us the present value of the firm in theory!

Cash Flows, Not Profits or Dividends

Now, it is important to realize that we are discounting cash flows. We aren't discounting profits. This is because, profits are subjective. Management has significant discretion over the amount of profits that it wants to report. Also, profits really are an opinion. Dividends on the other hand are just monies paid out to shareholders. Dividends do not reflect profitability. A company could go into loss but still pay a dividend. In fact, many companies do that! So, dividends also aren't really a good barometer to judge the performance of a company.

Besides, the company can invest cash for further growth of their business. So the opportunity cost for the company really begins when cash comes in the door. Hence cash flow is used and hence the model is called discounted cash flow model.

The Problem with Perpetual Existence

Now, we earlier stated that the process begins with estimating the life of the company. Here is a real problem! The company does not have a finite life at all. The company is a legal person created by law. Legally they have an infinite life. This feature of a corporation is called perpetual succession. Now, this poses real problems when it comes to valuing shares because this means that our cash flows are expected to go on till eternity! How can you value an infinite series of future cash flow payments? Well, we cannot until we make some assumptions. Those assumptions are discussed below.

Two Step Model

To arrive at a value for a company's stock, we need to split the calculation into two parts. The first part is called the "horizon period". This is the period for which we will estimate the cash flows with a good degree of precision. This period is generally 4 to 7 years and is the choice that an analyst needs to make. Since this is a finite series of cash flows we can easily discount it and come up with a finite value.

The remaining part of the life of the stock is considered to be a growing perpetuity. So the analyst must make an assumption regarding the constant rate of return that is assumed to be earned by the company till perpetuity. This constant rate must be less than the discounting rate. This makes it an infinitely decreasing series. Mathematically we can come up with a finite value for an infinite set of numbers if their value is decreasing. Hence, we can come up with a finite value for the perpetuity as well.

In the end we need to add up the value of the horizon period as well as the perpetuity to get the discounted value of cash flows. This is how the discounted cash flow model is used to arrive at a stock valuation.

Assumptions Made During Stock Price Valuation

Estimating the value of equity stock of a company is not an easy proposition. This is because while estimating the stock price, all the data required to be used in the formula is not easily available. This is because the data is subjective. It is really the analysts call on what they believe about the company, its future and based on it what numbers they input in the formula.

Also, slightly different numbers used in the formula give vastly different results. Hence, an analyst must have a strong basis to use any number as an input to the stock valuation formula. Here are some of the common assumptions that will have to be made by the analyst during the stock valuation exercise:

Horizon Period

As we learned in the previous One that stock valuation happens in two stages. The first stage is the horizon period for which exact cash flows are estimated. Beyond the horizon period, the stock is considered to be a growing perpetuity and its value is estimated. But the question is "How big or small should the horizon period be and why?" We need to understand that the answer to this is not factual or based in proof. Rather, the answer is based on subjectivity and convention. It is therefore entirely up to the analyst to decide what the horizon period should be? An investor, however must be aware that changing the horizon period has massive effects on the stock valuation and must therefore watch out for the same.

Constant Growth Rate

After the horizon period is over, the stock is considered to be a growing perpetuity. This means that it will continue growing at a constant rate for the rest of its perpetual life. This rate must be less than the required rate of return or else the answer we will receive will be infinite since it will no longer be a decreasing infinite series.

But, then what should that constant rate of growth be? This is again a matter of great subjectivity. Once again the analyst has a high level of discretion in this decision. Also, this assumption is extremely important because the value of the perpetuity accounts for almost two thirds of the stock price in most cases. A wrong assumption here can therefore give a significantly higher or lower stock price.

Cost of Capital

Apart from the expected returns to be realized from the venture, there is also a great deal of subjectivity regarding the riskiness that is involved in each case. It is obviously difficult to compare the riskiness across industries and across companies. It is for this reason that estimating the cost of capital becomes relatively difficult. The market is efficient in pricing risk to a large extent. The cost of equity capital is calculated using data from the market from the past few years. But once again, the riskiness can be very different depending on whether we select data for the past 10 years or for the past 15 years. This makes it a subjective decision too!

Future Growth Opportunities

Also, the cash flows in the horizon period are estimated based on what the analyst thinks the future looks like in the next 5 to 7 years or whatever is the chosen horizon period. But, it is important to know that these estimates rarely end up being accurate. Consider the fact that business cycles are largely unpredictable, and so are the moves by the competition and we understand why we can't be relatively certain even about the future in the short and medium term.

The bottom line therefore is that any stock valuation is like a building which is standing on the pillars of its assumptions. A good investor will therefore first investigate the soundness and reasonableness of its assumptions before deciding whether or not the stock valuation is fair.

What is Cost of Equity ? - Meaning and Concept

Theoretical Concept

The cost of equity concept is very important when it comes to valuing shares on the stock market. Equity, like all other investment classes expects a compensation to be paid to its investors. The problem however is that unlike debt and other classes the cost of equity is never really straightforward. You can look at the interest rates that you are paying and you will straight away know what the cost of debt for your company is. However, the cost of equity is implied. Equity holders take the residual value that has been left from the profits. So it is not directly available.

However, for valuation purposes, the cost of equity is required. Without having the cost of equity and adding it to the discount rate, we will use a lower discount rate that does not reflect the riskiness of the investment. This may lead to selection of the wrong investments. So, this One provides a basis about how we can calculate the cost of equity.

There are two methods to calculating the cost of equity. One is the method that we are about to discuss now and the other is called the "Capital Asset Pricing Model". That will be discussed in a later One in the same module.

Assumes Market Price Is Correct:

In this method, we will begin with the assumption that the market price is correct. Now, we already know that the market price is nothing but the discounted value of all the future dividends that the company will pay, we can consider the market price to be the value of a perpetuity. Using the perpetuity formula, we can then express the market price as:

Market Price = Dividend (Next Year) / Discount Rate

Growing Perpetuity:

However in a perpetuity the payments remain the same throughout the life of the asset. So by using this formula, we are making the assumption that the dividends paid out across the life of the stock will be the same. Now, we know for sure that is not the case. In reality, the dividends usually grow over time. So we can use the formula for a growing perpetuity. That should give us a better approximation.

Market Price = Dividend (Next Year) / (Discount Rate – Growth Rate)

Rearrange The Formula:

So, now we can re-arrange this formula and solve for the discount rate. The discount rate is our cost of capital and it will be the output from the rearranged formula.

Discount Rate = {Dividend (Next Year) / Market Price} + Growth Rate

So, here it is! We have derived a formula which tells us an estimate of what is the cost of equity that is being demanded from this company by the market.

Estimating the Growth Rate:

Since growth rate is an important component of this formula, we need to ensure that we are using the correct growth rate. We can conduct this estimation in a couple of ways.

- Firstly, we could just calculate what the growth rate has been in the past. We can understand the trend and then use the same growth rate assuming that what happened in the past will continue in the future.

- Alternatively, we could make a more educated guess. The growth rate of dividend next year is dependent on the amount that we invest in the business this year and the rate of return we should earn on that investment right. So growth rate can be derived by using this formula:

Growth Rate = Plowback Ratio * ROE

Plowback ratio is the amount that the company expects to retain in the business whereas ROE is the return on equity that the company historically earns on its equity investments.

It may seem a little complex and full of formulas at the beginning. But there really is just one formula. Other formulas are used to derive the components that will be used in that single formula. So calculating the Cost of Equity that is being implied by the market price shouldn't really be that difficult.

What is Payback Period ?

We have earlier discussed the fact that Net present Value (NPV) is considered to be the gold standard when it comes to financial decision making. If a project has an NPV greater than zero then it is supposed to be a financially viable project and the firm must invest its resources towards that project, if not the project should be rejected.

But NPV is not the only metric that we can use to come to this decision regarding accepting or rejecting a project. Payback period is another such metric. In this One we will discuss about the conceptual foundation of payback period and then we shall see its drawbacks.

Payback Period

Payback period basically pays attention to the speed at which the initial investment made in a project will be recovered by subsequent cash flows. The project which helps recoup the investment the fastest is considered to be the best project and that is the project that the firm must dedicate its resources to.

Example:

Let's say that there are 2 projects A and B. Both require an equal outlay of $2000. Project A pays back $1500 in year 1, $500 in year 2 and $500 in year 3. Project B on the other hand pays $750 for 4 consecutive years.

So, now in this case if we were to use the payback period rule. We could consider the period in which the initial $2000 investment is recovered. In case of Project A, we recover it in 2 years whereas in case of Project B it requires 3 years. So according to the payback rule, Project A is better than Project B and the company must clearly devote its finite resources to Project A before it decides whether or not to undertake Project B.

Now, this decision could be wrong because of a couple of reasons:

1. Firstly, we are only calculating the time it requires to recoup the initial investment we made. In doing so, we are disregarding all the cash flows that occur after the initial investment has been fully recouped. In the above example, Project A pays out a total of $2500, whereas Project B pays out a total of $3000 over its lifetime. Yet, our decision criteria made us disregard this and choose Project A. So using payback period as your decision criteria could lead you to disregard projects that pay slower but would in fact pay more and therefore add more value to the firm.

2. Secondly, the money value of all the cash flows happening in all of the years was considered to be the same. This means that we are implicitly saying that the value of a dollar received in year 1 is the same as the value received in year 4 or 5. We know this is not the case. The real value of the money keeps on declining as time passes. Besides,

we also ignore the opportunity cost of the money that we could have earned if we received the cash earlier.

To overcome the second limitation of ignoring the time value of money, a modified measure of payback period called the discounted payback period is often used. This measure still does not overcome the fact that payback period does not account for the cash flows after the initial investment has been recouped. This is the reason why payback period is not a perfect metric and why NPV leads to better decisions.

What is Internal Rate of Return (IRR) ?

The Internal Rate of Return (IRR) is another very important metric that can be used to determine whether or not a company must invest its resources in a project. If the company does decide to invest its resources in all the projects then the IRR can help us understand what should be the priority of these projects for the company.

What Is Internal Rate of Return (IRR) ?

Let's understand Internal Rate of Return (IRR) with the help of an example. Let's say that we have an investment that pays $10 on a $100 investment. So, we can clearly see that the rate of return is 10%. This means 10% of the money invested will be recouped every single time period. But this calculation was simple because there was only one return we received and we just had to calculate its size as compared to the original investment.

Now, consider the fact that for the same $100 investment, you are going to receive $20 for the first 2 years, $30 for the next 2 years and $50 in the 5th year. So what would be the rate of return for this investment? So here we are taking a complex schedule of cash outflows and inflows and we are basically coming up with a single rate that describes the rate of return. In the above example the rate of return is 13%.

This means that if we invested $100 and got a consistent rate of interest which was compounded at 13%, then that investment would be equivalent to the above investment. The above investment provides the same return as that of a bond with an annual coupon of 13%. This is the Internal Rate of Return (IRR) of the investment.

The calculation of Internal Rate of Return (IRR) with a formula is very complex and is never used in practice. We generally use financial calculators or MS Excel both of which have inbuilt IRR functions to find out the IRR.

Relationship between the IRR and the NPV

The relationship between the IRR and the NPV is very important. In fact, it could be the defining characteristic of IRR. IRR is the rate at which NPV of the project is zero. This is clearly intuitive. Consider the fact that the rate of growth of your investment and the discount rate both will be the same in this case. Therefore they will nullify each other and the NPV will be zero at IRR.

The Internal Rate of Return (IRR) Rule

The rule pertaining to the IRR is simple. A company must decide a hurdle IRR rate. Let's say the hurdle rate is 10%. So, the company must then choose investments that pay over 10% and must reject investments that pay less than 10%. In the above example 13% is greater than 10% and hence the investment must be selected. In case the company wants to choose between 2 projects both of which have more than 10% return, then the one with the higher Internal Rate of Return (IRR) must be selected.

The IRR metric is also flawed. But its flaws are smaller as compared to the payback period method. It is for this reason that many companies do in fact use the IRR method to decide amongst investments. It is a little bit more intuitive to use. Its flaws have been discussed in the forthcoming One.

Problems With Using Internal Rate of Return (IRR) for Investment Decision Making

In the past One we discussed about the concept of internal rate of return. We discussed how it could be used to make proficient investment decisions. In this One we will see the drawbacks and pitfalls of the Internal Rate of Return (IRR) number. We will see how these problems make it a number that must be handled with care and why decisions based entirely on the IRR rule may not be good for the firm. The problems with Internal Rate of Return (IRR) are as follows:

Problem #1: Multiple Rates of Return

The Internal Rate of Return (IRR) is a complex mathematical formula. It takes inputs, solves a complex equation and gives out an answer. However, these answers are not correct all the time. There are some cases in which the cash flow pattern is such that the calculation of IRR actually ends up giving multiple rates. So instead of having one IRR, we would then have multiple IRR's. Sometimes the IRR number can even go in the negative indicating that the firm is actually losing value. Although, we know that this is not the case in reality.

The thumb rule is that if the cash flow patterns change signs more than One then the firm sees more than 1 IRR. These numbers are therefore not wholly accurate. They are simply the result of a mathematical error of a complex formula. In such cases, using the NPV is a better choice.

And most projects that firms have to choose from will usually have cash flows which change signs many times. Sometimes there is a maintenance outlay required during the later life of the project. Sometimes disposing off the waste at the end of the project requires an outlay in the end. In each of these cases, Internal Rate of Return (IRR) is not a good basis for decisions.

Problem # 2: Multiple Discount Rates

Even if the cash flow does not change signs in the middle of the project, the IRR could still be very difficult to compute and implement in reality. We must only invest if the IRR is greater than the opportunity cost of capital. But, here we are just discussing one opportunity cost of capital. Time value of money tells us that there are in fact several opportunity costs of capital, changing each year because of the effect of increasing number of years.

So, to use the IRR rule in such a case we have two choices:

1. We can use the IRR and the discount rate values for each year and make a decision
2. Alternatively, we can compute a weighted average Internal Rate of Return (IRR) and use that to make the decision

Either ways, it becomes a mathematical hassle. This is both difficult to comprehend as well as difficult to compute. It is for this reason that firms usually prefer the net present value (NPV) rule to the Internal Rate of Return (IRR) rule.

Capital Rationing and Profitability Index

In the previous few One we have come across different metrics that can be used to choose amongst competing projects. These metrics help the company identify the project that will add maximum value and helps make informed decisions to maximize the wealth of the firm. We saw how the NPV rule was better than IRR and the profitability index and how decisions based on NPV are supposedly more accurate.

However, we need to understand that there is a difference between how the NPV rule is stated in text books and how it is applied in real life worldwide. This difference arises because when we consider capital budgeting, we are working under the fundamental assumption that the firm has access to efficient markets. This means that if the required rate of return is greater than the opportunity cost of capital, or if the project has an NPV greater than zero, the firm can always finance its projects by raising money from the markets even if it doesn't have any. Thus for practical purposes, the money at the firms disposal is unlimited.

However, in reality this may not be the case. True, that firms can always raise money and bigger firms can raise as much funds as they want to, but many times firms themselves place restrictions on the amount of fund raising that they undertake.

These restrictions could be placed because of the following reasons:

- Raising more equity could dilute the existing ownership interest
- There may be debt covenants preventing the firm from raising more debt
- Raising more funds either by debt or equity may make the firm appear riskier and may take the cost of capital even higher

This restriction placed on the amount of capital that the company has, nullifies the assumption inherent in capital budgeting. Thus, what happens in real life is a slightly modified version of capital budgeting. Financial analysts have a name for this. They call it "Capital Rationing".

So **capital rationing is nothing but capital budgeting with modified rules**. Now instead of choosing every project that has an NPV greater than zero, the firm uses a different approach. All projects with a positive NPV qualify for a possible investment. These projects are then ranked according to their attractiveness. The firm then invests in the top3 or top 5 projects (based on their resources). So, here a finite amount of capital is being rationed amongst projects as opposed to an infinite capital assumption.

Profitability Index

But, how does the firm decide which projects are the most attractive? Simply ranking the projects with higher NPV will be incorrect. This is because we are not paying attention to the input we are putting in. We are simply paying attention to the output which is obviously incorrect. What if a project with a slightly higher NPV requires double the investment as compared to another project? Is it still a good bet?

Obviously not and to solve this problem and ration capital effectively, companies have come up with a metric called the Profitability Index. The profitability index is nothing but the NPV of the project divided by the amount of its investment.

Profitability Index = NPV / Investment

So we are simply looking at the NPV amount per dollar of investment. Projects with highest NPV per dollar of investment are considered more attractive and the investment dollars are first allocated to them so that the returns of the firm are maximized.

Types of Capital Rationing

As discussed in the previous One, capital rationing is a form of capital budgeting. In capital rationing we change the unlimited capital assumption of capital budgeting and we try to choose projects with the finite capital that we have on hand. This finite capital may be in the form of capital that the firm already has or it may be in the form of a decision to raise a limited amount of capital in the future. Either way, the amount of capital available at the company's disposal for decision making is finite and it is known. There are two types of capital rationing. They have been explained in this One:

Soft Rationing

Soft rationing is when the firm itself limits the amount of capital that is going to be used for investment decisions in a given time period. This could happen because of a variety of reasons:

- The promoters may be of the opinion that if they raise too much capital too soon, they may lose control of the firm's operations. Rather, they may want to raise capital slowly over a longer period of time and retain control. Besides if the firm is constantly demonstrating a high level of proficiency in generating returns it may get a better valuation when it raises capital in the future.

- Also, the management may be worried that if too much debt is raised it may exponentially increase the risk raising the opportunity cost of capital. Most firms have written guidelines regarding the amount of debt and capital that they plan to raise to keep their liquidity and solvency ratios intact and these guidelines are usually adhered to.

- Thirdly, many managers believe that they are taking decisions under imperfect market conditions i.e. they do not know about the opportunities available in the future. Maybe a project with a better rate of return can be found in the future or maybe the cost of capital may decline in the future. Either way, the firm must conserve some capital for the opportunities that may arise in the future. After all raising capital takes time and this may lead to a missed opportunity!

This type of rationing is called soft because it is the firm's internal decision. They can change or modify it in the future if they think that it is in their best interest to do so.

Also, companies usually implement this kind of rationing on a department basis. From a master investment budget, departmental investment budgets are drawn and each department is asked to choose projects on the basis of funds allocated. Only in case of an extremely attractive project are the departmental restrictions on capital investments compromised.

Hard Rationing

Hard rationing, on the other hand, is the limitation on capital that is forced by factors external to the firm. This could also be due to a variety of reasons:

- For instance, a young startup firm may not be able to raise capital no matter how lucrative their project looks on paper and how high the projected returns may be.
- Even medium sized companies are dependent on banks and institutional investors for their capital as many of them are not listed on the stock exchange or do not have enough credibility to sell debt to the common people.
- Lastly, large sized companies may face restrictions by existing investors such as banks who place an upper limit on the amount of debt that can be issued before they make a loan. Such covenants are laid down to ensure that the company does not borrow excessively increasing risk and jeopardizing the investments of old lenders.

So hard rationing arises because of market imperfections and because of limitations created by external parties.

Estimating Project Cash Flows: Part 1

Prima facie, capital budgeting may seem like a very simple task. After all, it has just 3 steps. The first is to find the cash flows, the second is to find the appropriate discount rate that represents the time value and riskiness of those cash flows and the third step is to use both these inputs and discount the cash flows at the chosen rate.

However, in practice it is not that straightforward. There are many complications that arise during the process. Complications usually arise because neither of the variables that we are using in the projection is certain. We are therefore, at best choosing estimates. Deciding whether we have the right estimates is very important. A slight change could bring about a completely different valuation. **In this One, we will first see how we can derive cash flows from accounting profits and then we shall have a closer look at some of the complications that may arise in the process of estimating cash flows**.

Deriving Accounting Profits from Cash Flows

Capital budgeting is completely dependent upon cash flows. It is not concerned with the accounting profits of a project. Yet, most of the times analysts will have financial statements that talk about the accounting profit. So, they have to derive the cash flows from the accounting profit. This can be done by undoing the two adjustments that accountants make to come at the profit:

1. Accountants count income in the period it is earned. As opposed to this, cash flow needs to be accounted for in the period that it was received. Hence the numbers need to be adjusted.

2. Also, accountants segregate the cash outflows into expenses and asset creation. But when you consider cash, it's just an outflow. So once again, this assumption also needs to be undone while computing the cash flows that need to be discounted.

Only Incremental Cash Flows

Secondly, it is important to consider each project as a separate investment and we must consider only the incremental cash flows that arise as a result of this investment decision. Consider for example that we decide to open up a restaurant in a property that we have already rented out for $10,000 a year. The cash inflow from this restaurant is expected to be $25,000 a year.

In this case, even though the nominal value of cash inflows is $25,000, in reality we are earning just $15,000 of additional money. Hence we will use $15,000 for our cash-flow calculations and not $25,000. The key is to consider the value of your firm with and without the investment. The idea is to look at both possible scenarios and decide which one we want to be in.

This part can be counter-intuitive for many people. But remember that we are only considered with the additional dollars that we will make as a result of this investment. Why should we consider what we are already earning from past projects into consideration to decide whether or not we should invest in the next one?

Incidental Effects

Also, it is important to consider the incidental effects of some projects. In theory, projects work in isolation. But we know for a fact that in reality that is not the case. The fate of many projects is usually interconnected.

Let's say a car company is deciding whether or not it should introduce a new model of car. Now, let's also say that this new model's sales will decrease the sale of another model produced by the same company. They will cause the sale of the old model to drop by $12,000.

So, while calculating the cash inflows from the new model, we must subtract $12,000 from it. This is because without the project the company has the $12,000 but with the project, the company stands to lose $12,000. It may make additional money but $12,000 is an incidental cost that is being paid to undertake this project.

Hence, to gauge the real value of the project, incidental costs must also be taken into account.

Estimating Project Cash Flows: Part 1

Prima facie, capital budgeting may seem like a very simple task. After all, it has just 3 steps. The first is to find the cash flows, the second is to find the appropriate discount rate that represents the time value and riskiness of those cash flows and the third step is to use both these inputs and discount the cash flows at the chosen rate.

However, in practice it is not that straightforward. There are many complications that arise during the process. Complications usually arise because neither of the variables that we are using in the projection is certain. We are therefore, at best choosing estimates. Deciding whether we have the right estimates is very important. A slight change could bring about a completely different valuation. **In this One, we will first see how we can derive cash flows from accounting profits and then we shall have a closer look at some of the complications that may arise in the process of estimating cash flows**.

Deriving Accounting Profits from Cash Flows

Capital budgeting is completely dependent upon cash flows. It is not concerned with the accounting profits of a project. Yet, most of the times analysts will have financial statements that talk about the accounting profit. So, they have to derive the cash flows from the accounting profit. This can be done by undoing the two adjustments that accountants make to come at the profit:

1. Accountants count income in the period it is earned. As opposed to this, cash flow needs to be accounted for in the period that it was received. Hence the numbers need to be adjusted.

2. Also, accountants segregate the cash outflows into expenses and asset creation. But when you consider cash, it's just an outflow. So once again, this assumption also needs to be undone while computing the cash flows that need to be discounted.

Only Incremental Cash Flows

Secondly, it is important to consider each project as a separate investment and we must consider only the incremental cash flows that arise as a result of this investment decision. Consider for example that we decide to open up a restaurant in a property that we have already rented out for $10,000 a year. The cash inflow from this restaurant is expected to be $25,000 a year.

In this case, even though the nominal value of cash inflows is $25,000, in reality we are earning just $15,000 of additional money. Hence we will use $15,000 for our cash-flow calculations and not $25,000. The key is to consider the value of your firm with and without the investment. The idea is to look at both possible scenarios and decide which one we want to be in.

This part can be counter-intuitive for many people. But remember that we are only considered with the additional dollars that we will make as a result of this investment. Why should we consider what we are already earning from past projects into consideration to decide whether or not we should invest in the next one?

Incidental Effects

Also, it is important to consider the incidental effects of some projects. In theory, projects work in isolation. But we know for a fact that in reality that is not the case. The fate of many projects is usually interconnected.

Let's say a car company is deciding whether or not it should introduce a new model of car. Now, let's also say that this new model's sales will decrease the sale of another model produced by the same company. They will cause the sale of the old model to drop by $12,000.

So, while calculating the cash inflows from the new model, we must subtract $12,000 from it. This is because without the project the company has the $12,000 but with the project, the company stands to lose $12,000. It may make additional money but $12,000 is an incidental cost that is being paid to undertake this project.

Hence, to gauge the real value of the project, incidental costs must also be taken into account.

Estimating Project Cash Flows: Part 2

We have seen in the previous One that estimating cash flows can be quite confusing and counterintuitive. This is not because they are difficult to calculate. It is just because the course of action taken is opposite to what would have been taken in the case of accounting. Accounting is concerned with matching expenses to the relevant period. But in cash flow analysis, the matching concept doesn't apply! Also, implicit costs are sometimes used in calculation. This One will look forward at clearing some more of those confusions.

Opportunity Costs

Opportunity costs are notional or implicit costs. This means that the money never actually leaves our pockets. They are not expenditures in reality. Rather, they are fictional expenditures. Opportunity cost is the value of the next best alternative which has been foregone to allocate resources to a project.

Let's consider a scare resource i.e. your time. Let's say reading and watching movies are the only two possible alternative uses that you could have made of your time. So, each time you watch a movie, you are not reading and each time you read, you are not watching a movie. Therefore, reading is the opportunity cost (next best alternative) of movies and vice versa.

Similarly, when the firm invests its money in project A, it is automatically not investing its money in project B. So the returns of project B (which we did not earn in reality) have to be foregone. The objective of capital budgeting is to ensure that the company can make the best possible choice when faced between conflicting alternatives. So it is imperative that the alternative must be accounted for.

It is for this reason that the opportunity cost of project B should be taken in to account while deciding whether or not project A must be undertaken. Thus, opportunity costs which are not a type of explicit cost and which would have simply been ignored in accounting are being used in cash flow calculations for corporate finance.

Estimating this opportunity cost can sometimes be very difficult. If there is a ready market for the asset for which we need to know the opportunity cost then we can use the prices being reflected in the market as a barometer. However, if no ready market exists, the prices have to be estimated. This can sometimes be a problem. Companies can employ trained appraisers to help determine the saleable value which can be used as the opportunity cost.

Another important point is that the opportunity cost of Project A cannot have a value greater than A. If it has a value greater than A, then that project should be selected and A should become the next best alternative, isn't it?

Incremental Working Capital

Just like in case of capital expenditures, we will only consider the incremental cash outflow which results from an increase in working capital because of the new projects. The old working capital should obviously be excluded from any calculations since it will remain unaffected whether or not the project is undertaken.

We need to be careful to calculate the amount of working capital that will be required. This is because the working capital will usually be simply rolled over from one period to another. So, we invest one amount and it keeps rolling on till the end of the project and seldom requires more cash infusions. Many times, this amount may be left over at the end of the project and it is added to the cash inflows while calculating the Net Present Value. Once again, we are doing the counterintuitive. In accounting working capital was always an expense. Here, at the end of the project, we may add it to the cash inflow!

There are still some more peculiarities about cash flow calculations which we will consider in the next One.

Estimating Project Cash Flows: Part 3

Continuing from the previous twice, we will look at some more counterintuitive steps that need to be taken to calculate the cash flows which should then be discounted to arrive at the worth of the project. This One will cover the concepts of how sunk costs should be treated as well as how allocated overheads may at times be different from the overhead value that we have to use in our cash flow calculations.

Sunk Costs

Sunk costs are expenses that have happened in the past that will not be affected by the current decision. The second part is very important. Defining sunk costs just as expenses that have happened in the past would be inappropriate if our current decisions affect them.

Consider a case when the firm has already spent $1 million on a project. However, the project has turned out to be unsuccessful till date. It has not churned out any positive cash flows till date. Now, the company is faced with a choice. The choice is whether it should invest more in the project that it has spent $1million on or whether it should pursue a new project.

The important point is not the answer. The important point here is the thought process that will be used to arrive at the answer. The correct thought process understands that $1m already spent has nothing to do with the new choice they are faced with. The incremental dollars also deserve their best use and hence the decision must be taken solely on the basis of NPV of additional money that is going to be spent. The old $1m is not affected by the decision that has to be taken now. Hence it is irrelevant and must be completely ignored during the decision making.

Allocated Overhead Costs

Overheads are costs that cannot be assigned to any activity directly. Assigning them within the company's different departments and projects therefore becomes a problem. This problem is solved by accountants through the concept of allocation. Since the track of where the money was actually spent cannot be kept, accountants assume a basis and costs are allocated on that basis. The problem is that these allocated costs may not be good for our cash flow analysis purpose.

For instance, consider the fact that there are 3 departments A, B and C. The total overheads of the company now are $100. The allocation base used is labor hours and the proportion in which these costs are split is 2:2:1. Hence A, B and C have allocated overheads of $40, $40 and $20.

Now, consider what happens when the 4th department is introduced. The fourth department has an additional overhead cost of $20 taking total overheads to $120. However, based on the labor hours basis the new ratio is 3:3:1:3

Based on this the overheads allocated to department A, B, C and D are $36, $36, $12 and $36 respectively. So, for department D, we have an allocated overheads cost of $36 as opposed to incremental overheads cost of $20. Since, cash flow analysis is all about incremental costs, it is essential that we take into consideration the incremental costs and not the allocated costs while performing the calculations.

Capital Budgeting and the Treatment of Inflation

Forecasts Spread Over a Period of Time

Inflation is an ever persistent condition in today's economy. The purchasing power of money has been reducing year after year for decades now. Apart from the occasional recession where money may gain real value, the usual case is a loss of value. Investors are investing money today. They want to be compensated for the inflation and still get a return over and above it. This simply means that they want to gain value in real terms.

It is important for us to understand this while coming up with our cash flow estimations. This is because projects never give all of their cash flows in the same period. Cash flows from projects are usually spread out over many years, even decades. The treatment of inflation therefore becomes very important to come up with the correct value. Minor changes in the assumptions about inflation are capable of producing massive changes in the expected return from the project. A viable project may become unviable simply by tweaking the inflation numbers a little bit. This One will explain how inflation needs to be treated while performing these calculations:

Inflation Affects Different Components Differently

First, we need to understand that inflation never affects all the components of the income statement uniformly. Therefore assuming a uniform rate for all the components might give theoretically correct answers, but in practical life it will be a blunder. For instance, consider the fact that labor costs will go up every year. Employees usually expect to be paid a hike every year. Also, the cost of raw materials is expected to go up every year. Tax rates change every year. However, the increase in sales price cannot match these changes. It will usually be either more or less than the percentage change in other components. Sales price is market driven and we can't just raise it without incurring any loss.

The bottom line therefore is that a good analyst will study the past record of each of these components in terms of their inflationary tendency. He/she will then try to make forecasts about the future trends that are likely to prevail. Based on this, every component should have its own unique rate of inflation. In more detailed analyses, inflation forecasts will vary year to year depending on how the analyst predicts the economy to behave.

The Golden Rule

The golden rule when it comes to capital budgeting and inflation is that we must be consistent in our treatments of inflation. The keyword is consistency. If we have real cash-flows, we must discount them at the real rate of interest. On the other hand, if we have nominal cash flows (usually the case), we must discount them at a nominal rate of interest. This might seem obvious, but is a common mistake to use the wrong discount rate.

We have earlier studied a formula to convert nominal rates to real rates and vice versa. The formula is as follows:

(1 + nominal rate) = (1 + real rate) * (1 + inflation rate)

An Approximation to the Golden Rule

This formula maybe required if you are doing precise calculations. If the intent is to come up with an approximate figure, simple back of the hand calculations will suffice. Hence, if the nominal rate is stated at 12% and the inflation rate is stated at 4%, it is a reasonable assumption to assume 4% as the real rate of return. Obviously the resultant numbers will not be precise but they will provide a good approximation which is exactly what is required sometimes.

Despite all the forecasting techniques and calculations, analysts are usually way off the mark when it comes to predicting inflation rates. This is not because of their shortcomings but rather because of the unpredictable nature of the economy. Nonetheless, they try to refine their methods time and again in the quest to get the inflation numbers right.

Capital Budgeting and Depreciation

Depreciation is an important concept in capital budgeting. This is because it is a non cash expense and ideally should not have any effect on the cash flows. This is the reason why it is added back during cash flow calculations. Since the amount of depreciation never actually left our bank account in the form of expenses, we still have it in cash. So prima facie, it may appear like depreciation had no effect whatsoever. First, we deducted it while calculating the net income in the income statement. Then we added the same amount back while calculating cash flows, thus nullifying its effect.

However, there is more to depreciation. Depreciation affects cash flows in an indirect manner. The effect of the same has been described in this One.

Depreciation and Taxation

It is true that depreciation is a non cash expense. However depreciation is tax deductible. So the amount of depreciation we pay affects the amount of taxes we pay. Remember while calculating net income we remove the depreciation and amortization figure from EBIDTA to arrive at Profit before Tax. This is the amount on which tax is levied and we get the Profit after Tax figure.

Therefore, the higher the depreciation amount, the lower will be the taxable profit and as a result the lower will be the amount paid as tax. Depreciation, therefore indirectly affects the cash flow by reducing the amount of taxes paid and hence a high depreciation may actually have a positive impact on the cash flows!

Depreciation Tax Shield

The exact amount of taxes that were reduced because of depreciation can be calculated. This is known as the depreciation tax shield. Let's understand this with the help of an example:

	With Depreciation	Without Depreciation
EBIDTA	$2000	$2000
Depreciation	$500	$0
PBT	$1500	$2000
Tax @ 40%	$600	$800
PAT	$900	$1200

Now, as we can see that when we consider depreciation the tax paid is lower by $200 i.e. we pay $600 in taxes as opposed to $800. Therefore, $200 is the tax shield. However, we need not go through the entire calculation to come up with the amount of the tax shield.

Shortcut to Determine the Amount of the Tax Shield

The calculation can be simplified. We can consider that for every $1 that we have in depreciation, we have saved $0.40 in taxes. Thus to find out the amount of the tax shield all we need to do is multiply the amount of total depreciation by the ongoing tax rate. Consider for example $500 * 0.40. This is equal to $200, which is the exact amount we derived from the lengthy calculation above.

We need to understand that the tax shield amount will vary with the depreciation amount. So, accelerated depreciation methods will provide a higher tax shield upfront as compared to straight line methods. Also, since we are going to discount the values of these tax shields, the concept of time value of money applies. It is for this reason that accelerated method of depreciation will be preferred to straight line methods.

Equivalent Annual Costs

In the previous One we have seen how we can convert a possible future stream of cash flows to its present value today to make investment decisions. We choose amongst competing projects and the one with the highest NPV is usually selected. But sometimes this may not be the appropriate thing to do.

Example:

Consider the fact that the firm has to choose between two types of software to run its day to day operations. Now both these software are identical in the sense that they do the same job in pretty much the same manner. However, their costs are different and so is the duration of their licenses.

Software A costs $20,000 upfront, has a life of 4 years and the company will have to pay $2,500 as annual maintenance charge to the vendor. Software B, on the other hand costs $10,000 upfront requires an annual maintenance charge of $3000 for 3 years which is the duration of its license. Now, how does the company make a financially prudent decision and choose the more cost effective software.

The Problem:

Under normal circumstances, this would have been a pretty straightforward decision. The NPV of both the software could have been computed. Since we are talking about costs and not revenues, we would have selected the one with the lowest NPV. But there is a slight problem. The life of both the software is different. One will have to be renewed after 4 years while the other will have to be renewed after 3 years. So, the value of a future cash flow is contingent upon the decision that we make now. So, just looking at the NPV will be making a decision with incomplete information! The bottom line is that since the life of both these software is different, we can't really decide amongst them on the basis of NPV alone.

The Concept of Equivalent Annual Costs

Here we have the concept of equivalent annual costs to the rescue. The approach to the problem is simple if we look at it from this point of view. We now have lump sum NPV's which can be derived from the costs that have been stated above.

Assuming a discount rate of 10%, the NPV of software A and software B is $25,386 and $15,873 respectively. Our common sense approach would tell us to chose software B because of its lower NPV, but we just discussed why that would not be a wise choice because the duration of their licenses is different.

So, instead we start to view them as if we have taken these software on rent. This means that we will convert the NPV for software A into an annuity for 4 years, whereas that of software B for 3 years. By doing so, we will be able to bring both the costs down to an annual level. It is like choosing between software A or software B on the basis of which has the lowest annual rental payment. This nullifies the fact that they have different license durations.

Solution with Equivalent Annual Costs

Now, if we consider the present value of software A as $25,387, assume a 10% discount rate, the annual cost would be $8,008 for a period of 4 years.

Similarly, the present value of software B is $15,873, assuming the same 10% discount rate, the annual cost of software B would be $6,382 for a period of 3 years.

Since, the costs are annual, the number of years really do not matter. We are therefore facing a choice between an annual rent of $8,008 and $6,382. $6,382 is the lower rent and therefore software B is a more financially prudent choice.

Now, just to clarify, we are not taking the software on rent. We are buying it outright. The assumption regarding renting out the software was a metaphor to ensure that the concept of equivalent annual costs becomes easier to understand.

Separation of Investing and Financing Decisions

We have already seen that there are a lot of differences that arise between what we have learned in accounting and how we use it in corporate finance. The separation of financing and investing decisions is one such important concept. It is important because we have to make a very important adjustment based on this principle. That adjustment is the fact that we do not subtract interest costs while calculating the cash flows that a project will generate. This is different from accounting where we were used to subtracting the interest costs to calculate our income. So here we must remember that we have to exclude interest costs from our calculation. Failure to do so is one of the most common mistakes that are made by students.

Understanding What an Investing Decision and a Financing Decision Really Is?

When we take up a project, we really need to understand that we are making two decisions not one. The first decision is regarding the assets that we must invest in. This means that if we are opening up a restaurant we need to consider what the real estate would cost, what the improvements would cost to create the desired ambience, what the kitchen equipment would cost and so on. Then we must consider the returns that these investments will generate. This is the investing decision.

Now, the above investments could be done from spare cash that the company has, the company could sell more stock to raise the funds or they could even borrow to raise the funds for the project. How the company raises money for the project is an investment decision. Each of the above options has its own related costs. For instance debt will have interest cost, equity will have dividend cost etc. But that does not really change the cash flows of the project, does it?

The restaurant (investment) will generate the same returns regardless of how it is financed. Financing merely changes the people entitled to those profits. It does not change the amount of profits that are earned by the project.

The Procedure to Separate Investments and Financing Decisions

It is for this reason that we must first see the project without its financing costs to check whether it is viable. This simply means that the investment decision must be separated from the financing decision. Once the viability of the project has been established, the company can then conduct a separate analysis to determine how the project needs to be financed. The company can check whether an all debt financing is better than using all of their own cash or whether a combination of the two is required. However, this decision pertains to capital structure and not to capital budgeting.

Getting Creative with Capital Budgeting

From the past few One, it may seem like capital budgeting has a pre-determined procedure. All the possible scenarios that can occur have been thought of and appropriate solutions for all of them have already been developed. While this makes "capital budgeting" a good subject, it also removes the creativity from it. There is a general perception that jobs pertaining to finance and capital budgeting are boring and lack creative potential. As we shall see in this One, this is definitely not the case. The subject does provide room for ample creativity. Here are some examples:

Timing of the Project

Our NPV rule says that if a project has a positive NPV, it is financially viable. The NPV rule does not say that the project needs to be undertaken immediately. As many creative professionals have shown before, the NPV of a project can be magnified just by waiting for sometime before you execute it.

Consider the case of a building construction. You have conducted your analysis and it shows that given the cash inflows and outflows listed on your schedule, the project is a good bet. Does that mean you should execute it immediately? Well, this wouldn't be the case if you found out additional information.

What if you found out that the government was about to declare an area near your proposed building site to be a "tax-free zone" for corporations. You would obviously expect a lot of companies to set up their shop there and this would increase the property prices, isn't it?

Also, what if you find out that the government is about to create an underground train line linking that area to the centre of the city. Now, obviously it would make sense to wait, right? The NPV of the project is positive now. But it will be many times larger, if we waited for some more time. (Assuming that the information is credible)

So, a positive NPV does not mean that the project should be executed immediately. Any project always has two implicit options. One is to execute it right away and the other is to execute it at a later date. Many times projects with negative NPV turn around positive in a few years. The real task of the financial manager therefore is to be aware of this information that could affect their project and look into the future. What is in the present can be easily seen and discounted even by a computer!

Re-Engineering

Many times companies are faced with this decision regarding whether or not they must re-engineer the way in which they operate. This may include shutting down for a few days and then re-opening with completely different equipment, processes etc. These projects are usually viewed by financial managers as an all or nothing game. They will calculate the NPV for the entire project as a whole before they make a decision.

Now, creative financial managers on the other hand realize that it doesn't have to be an all or nothing game. They pick and choose parts of the project and work out with combinations. They will try and find out if it is in the best interest to execute the entire project now or would executing 25% at a time for the next 4 years lead to a higher NPV.

The real point here is that the goal is to maximize the NPV. There will be given scenarios which are known to everyone. The trick is to think about the project in terms of time, partial implementation etc which are not the scenarios people would commonly think of. Like in all other professions, a good financial manager is a creative financial manager. He/she will find ways and means of maximizing the NPV.

Companys Risk vs. Project Risk

In the past module, we concentrated on calculating the returns part of the project. All our One were focused on calculating cash flows and we saw the various special cases that arise while determining cash flows and determined how we must deal with them. This module is all about the other component i.e. risk. The cash flows are nominal figures. To determine the true value of the project, we need to find out an appropriate discount rate for our project. This One is a primer in this regard. It will clear out the first and the most prevalent confusion pertaining to discount rates.

Let's say that we have a company "A". At the present moment, the cost of capital for company A, with its existing projects is 12%. Company A is planning to undertake a new project. The cash flows have been determined. It is now time to discount them. What do you think? Would using a 12% discount rate be appropriate?

The answer is that it is not appropriate and here is the reason why:

Company's Risk

A company's risk is measured by the rate at which its cash flows are being discounted currently by the market. This is the company's cost of capital. The important thing to realize is that this cost reflects the riskiness of the projects that have been undertaken by the company in the past. So, if company A currently has 6 projects running, this discount rate of 12% is a measure of the riskiness of those 6 projects.

Project Risk

Project risk, on the other hand, is independent of company's risk. It doesn't really matter if Company A has a 12% discount rate. If the new project is considerably more risky than the past projects undertaken by A then the discount rate must reflect this additional risk. The project needs to be evaluated on its own merits. The discount factor must determine the riskiness of a probable future course of action rather than that of past actions.

What Happens if We Use The 12% Discount Rate?

The general tendency is to use the past discount rate for selecting future projects. However, this is an error and could lead to at least two big consequences for the company, if not more. The two mistakes are:

1. Firstly, since we are using a discount rate which may represent more or less risk than the project has, we may end up making the wrong choices. These wrong choices could be in two forms. We could overestimate the risk for a good project and reject it or we could underestimate the risk for a bad project and accept it. Obviously this will lead to loss of value in the long run.

2. Secondly, since the discount rate of the new project is considered in combination with that of the old project, we would be underestimating the risk for the company as a whole. The company is nothing but a portfolio of several different projects. By using the wrong discount rate for one project, we are actually using the wrong discount rate for the company as a whole!

The bottom line therefore is that the discount rate used must represent the risk of the project and not that of the company. This distinction is very subtle but very important.

How Governments around the World are Bankrupting Future Generations for Present Consumption

The Debt Bomb and its Implications

The world is in crisis and one of the reasons for that is the excessive debt held by people, companies, and countries. The west is especially hit hard because of the profligacy of the last three decades starting from the 1970s, which have resulted in a consumerist lifestyle, and an accumulation of debt at all levels of society. The acceleration of this trend during the 1990s and the 2000s with the inevitable implosion happening in 2008 meant that the world and particularly the west are sitting on a time bomb that can explode anytime. As people, companies, and countries in the west pay down the debt, they are faced with a choice of either curbing the present consumption and paying down the debt accumulated so far or taking on more debt to pay off the existing debt and bankrupting future generations. In other words, as all levels of society take on more debt to continue the present consumption, the situation is such that this debt has to be paid off sometime in the future and most likely, the future generations would be saddled with this debt. Like a head of the family who accumulates, debts and leaves to the future to pay it back, all levels of society in the west are continuing the present unsustainable way of living.

The Situation in the United States

For instance, the United States is embarking on increasing its present debt and taking on more debt to pay off in the future. Further, as there are many social welfare oriented schemes like Medicaid, Medicare, and Social Security that are entitled to be for the cause of social justice, the country has to budget for these entitlements as well so that the fabric of society is not ruptured. However, there are many experts in the United States who believe that the government must not honor its commitments to the elderly and the sick and instead, must give tax breaks for the rich and subsidies for the giant corporations. Coupled with the line of thinking that advocates more spending and more consumption, this line of action is a surefire recipe for disaster. The point here is that the accumulated debt would be passed on to future generations who would find that they have to do without subsidized education, less spending on social schemes, and have to pay more taxes to repay the debt that has been accumulated so far.

The Situation in Europe

The situation in Europe is slightly different, as the policymakers there have embarked on a debt reduction program by focusing on austerity. Of course, the existing debt is also being carried forward which means that in addition to cutbacks on social schemes and a general sense of lack of basic spending, they would also have to repay the debt. The point here is that the situation in Europe is more severe than in the United States, which for the moment is postponing the problem. However, there are many experts who believe that the US would face this "Tsunami of Debt" and the "Debt Bomb" pretty soon and that the day of reckoning cannot be postponed forever. The clear implication of this is that eventually the world would have to wake up and face the reality of low growth, more austerity, and more taxes along with sacrificing comforts to just get along. This means that there are tough choices ahead for the present generation and the generations to come and therefore, it is better for those who are graduating now or are taking up jobs to be aware of these facts.

Concluding Thoughts

Finally, the present generation can limit the damage done so far by living sustainably and trying to innovate and ensure that growth returns through inventive and creative solutions. The other alternative is to live through an economic depression that would impact their lives drastically.

Role of Credit Rating Agencies in Determining Attractiveness of Companies and Countries

How Credit Ratings Agencies Do their Job

When companies and countries need to borrow money from the market, there needs to be an agency that determines their creditworthiness or their ability to repay and be a source of good investment. Even for individuals when they apply for a loan, the banks and financial institutions assess their ability to repay and their soundness. For instance, when you apply for a home or an automobile loan or for a credit card, the bank has internal processes that determine whether you should be given the loan. Similarly, when companies and countries borrow, there are credit rating agencies that assign ratings to them to signal to the market about their creditworthiness. The difference between individuals, companies, and countries as far as rating agencies are concerned is the scale of borrowing and the depth of analysis. Whereas countries are rated on a whole host of parameters, companies are rated according to the assets they hold, the cash flow both future and current, and individuals according to their credit history. The point to note is that more often than not, lenders need independent agencies that assess the creditworthiness of the parties and this is where credit rating agencies come into the picture.

Accolades and Brickbats for Credit Ratings Agencies

Of course, **credit rating agencies have been the target of investors in recent times as they have been blamed for not assessing the risk and return of certain securities and loans as was the case during the subprime crisis when the agencies gave good ratings to the mortgages and the financial**

instruments built on top of them. Indeed, many credit rating agencies like Moody's, S&P, or Standard and Poor's were the matter of investigation by the regulators because they were perceived as being hand in glove with the banks. This is the reason why credit ratings agencies need to be independent and autonomous. Moreover, credit rating agencies have a lot of power as their negative ratings can mar the chances of companies and countries being unable to borrow at cheaper rates. In other words, when the rating of a company or a country is lowered, it loses access to market borrowings at cheaper rates and has to pay a premium to secure funds. This premium is the result of the increased risk that lenders take for lower rated companies and countries.

Proprietary Algorithms and Parameters for Rating

There are various parameters on which credit ratings agencies assess the creditworthiness. For countries, the bonds are rated according to the prevailing economic, political, and social situation as well as on previous financial history and future projections of growth. Each of these variables is assigned a weighting and the cumulative average is arrived at according to their importance. To arrive at the consolidated credit rating, the agencies have both objective and subjective means of analysis. The parameters described above are the objective One and the group or the assessors' taking the decision has a subjective parameter wherein they can use their judgment and decide accordingly. Further, companies are rated according to the growth projections and the cash flow situation as well as assets and outstanding liabilities. The point to note here is that the credit ratings agencies have proprietary algorithms and software that they have developed which they use to rate the financial instruments. Apart from this, there is something called the counterparty risk which each financial instrument bears and this is an important factor in determining the rating.

Closing Thoughts

Finally, credit ratings agencies are known to make errors of judgments as discussed earlier. However, they are also known for getting it right as evidenced during the debt ceiling debate in the United States in 2011 when the sovereign rating was lowered because the lawmakers in Congress and the Senate failed to arrive at a deal till the eleventh hour. Hence, the key take away from this One is that credit rating is an art as well as a science and hence, one must understand the entire process rather than touching upon it superficially.

Federal Reserve Announcement to Taper Quantitative Easing

Recent Financial and Economic Events

The stock markets around the world have dipped and currencies lost ground along with the bond market (the market for sovereign debt) showing signs of stress. This has happened over the last two weeks and particularly so in the last week as the Federal Reserve has announced that its bond buying program or Quantitative Easing would begin to taper off from the end of this year. If just an announcement by the Fed can cause so much of damage in the markets, imagine what would happen when the actual process ends with the Fed removing the liquidity. This nightmare scenario is keeping all financial professionals awake at night as they begin to assess the impact of the Fed's announcement on the markets around the world. The key aspect here is that the Federal Reserve from the time the financial crisis started has been pumping money into the bond markets and the market for mortgages thereby creating asset bubbles and flows of hot money to the emerging markets. In other words, by printing money, the Fed has been able to pump the markets, which have gotten used to easy money and boundless liquidity.

Is a Perfect Storm about to hit the Financial Markets ?

The other aspect here is that the balance sheets of almost all banks in the western world are full of toxic debt and hence, they need capital infusion to make up for the losses suffered by them because of the bursting of the real estate bubble. Further, the excess liquidity floating in the western world has made its way to the emerging markets like India where the hot money has created high equity prices and asset bubbles. Coupled with the fact that the Chinese economy is also contracting, these events have the potential to cause the next big crisis in the world. The ensuing liquidity crunch would leave the banks in the western world gasping for breath and the emerging markets witnessing a flight of dollars out of their markets. This is the reason for the steep fall in the value of many currencies of the emerging economies. Apart from this, the borrowing costs of governments seem to be going up because there is no confidence in the system with the central banks on the verge of losing control. All these conditions are creating a perfect storm in the financial world and therefore, it is in the interest of investors, professionals, and anyone who follows the business world to be prepared for any eventuality.

More Debt is not the answer to Existing Debt

While not getting completely into the solution mode, it needs to be mentioned that the way to salvaging the financial system would be to let the "Too Big to Fail" banks go under thereby creating conditions for a revival in the markets. The point here is that unless the banks that have toxic debt and have huge derivative positions are allowed to collapse, the present method of pumping money into them to prop them up would result in more debt being created to solve the problem of existing debt.

The clear implication of all these events is that there are hard times ahead for all stakeholders and especially for those who have taken mortgages or student debt to finance their homes or pay for their education. In this grim scenario, sacrifices are required and hardship to be borne as the world starts to pay down the existing debt and return to the debt levels of the pre crisis world.

Concluding Thoughts

In brief, the road ahead for the financial system around the world is perilous and therefore, it is better for professionals and students to reassess their careers and their education and evaluate the returns that they are getting on their investments. Unless there is some magical method by which debt can be written off and everyone starts afresh on a blank slate, the world is going to witness more financial volatility and economic chaos in the months to come.

How Do Funds Transfer Systems Work

Domestic Funds Transfer

It is common for individuals and entities to transfer funds to their friends, family, business partners, and associates. The way funds transfer works is opaque to the individual as he or she simply instructs the banks (or enables funds transfer when using online banking) and waits for confirmation from the other end about whether the funds have reached the beneficiary or not. Between the sender and the recipient lies an intricate network of financial intermediaries and relationships that underpin the funds transfer system. For most domestic funds transfers, the process is straightforward as the sender and the beneficiary are located in the same country and hence, all it takes for the bank is to notify the other bank about the transfer and acknowledge receipt of the funds. In this respect, domestic funds transfers work almost in the same way that check clearances work. The sender and the beneficiary "talk to each other" (as the jargon terms it) through the clearing house which means that the sending bank has to send the funds to the clearing house and the clearing bank (usually the central bank in each country) then deposits the money into the recipient bank which then credits the same to the customer's account.

International Funds Transfer

However, the funds transfer involving countries and continents is vastly more complex than the domestic funds transfer is. First, the sender has to issue instructions to his or her bank to transfer the money. Next, after the sender's bank ascertains that the customer has enough money in his account (after converting it into the foreign currency using the prevalent exchange rate) stars the process by sending the money to the correspondent bank that is authorized to transact internationally. After this, the intermediary debits the sender's bank account held with it and credits the corresponding bank in the foreign country, which has a banking relationship with it. In other words, both the intermediaries need to have accounts of each other in their banks, which would enable them to transfer the funds. Once the intermediaries transact and transfer funds this way, the final leg of the funds transfer happens which is through the intermediary in the foreign country crediting the account of the receiver bank with which the recipient has a banking relationship. After this, the receiver bank checks the credentials of the recipient and if everything is ok, credits the account of the recipient. This completes the funds transfer process.

The Criticality of Funds Transfer System to the Global Economy

The above descriptions of domestic and international funds transfers are just basic descriptions without too much jargon like nostro account, vostro account, and the SWIFT system of validating payments. These would be discussed in detail in subsequent One and it would suffice to state here that the financial web of relationships that enables international and domestic funds transfers has evolved over the years with the result that the present system handles complex, and humungous volumes of money every day. Indeed, it can be said that without the backbone of the international funds transfer network, the global economy would come to an immediate standstill. Especially when one considers the fact that with globalization, international money transfers have become enterprises involving Trillions of Dollars, the funds transfer systems in most multinational banks in financial hubs like New York, London, Singapore, and Sydney work around the clock and in a coordinated manner to make funds transfer possible. Therefore, the next time you transfer funds to your family members or business associates located in another country, you would have an idea of what it takes to complete your request.

Concluding Thoughts

Finally, as mentioned earlier, this One is the basic introduction to an important aspect of banking and further research can be done by visiting the SWIFT website and other manuals that contain details about how funds transfers work in the global economy.

The Importance of KYC (Know Your Customer) Norms and Procedures in Banking

Follow the Money Trail

In recent months, there has been a spate of disclosures around the world about how banks are compromising on customer identification procedures and are indulging in money laundering and other unsavory activities. From the US to India and the shadow banking system around the world including China, regulators have realized that unless they rein in the shady practices of banking, the result would be chaos and disorder. This is the reason why the regulators around the world have started clamping down on banks and asking them to foolproof their procedures. An important step in this direction is the directive to the banks to follow the KYC or the Know Your Customer norms and procedures through which the customers and their details can be recorded and stored so that in case of any wrongdoing, the law enforcers and the regulators would have the money trail leading to the individuals or entities. The key aspect about banking is that one must follow the money or in other words, investigate the money trail to see where it starts and where it ends. Once the money trail is established, it is easy to track down the culprits and this is the reason that banks must have accurate, reliable, and updated KYC norms in place for all customers.

The Uses and Misuses of KYC Norms

Having said that, it must be remembered that most banks use the KYC norms as an excuse to harass genuine customers and at the same time, indulge in unofficial activities. Therefore, the approach to following KYC norms is to insist on the same for all customers and especially those who have large sums on deposit as the scope for money laundering increases with these customers. On the other hand, they must not harass small depositors who anyway maintain less balance and whose activities can be monitored for suspicious transactions. The point here is that KYC norms should be used in conjunction with the monitoring of all accounts and the key principle that must be applied is that the norms are sacrosanct and at the same time, flexible enough to separate the genuine investors from the dubious One. Further, banks must ensure that high value transactions are monitored and insist on proper identification when customers deposit or withdraw huge sums of money. This is where proper KYC norms become useful as the contact information provided in the KYC database can be used by law enforcers and the regulators to track down the source and the destination of the money trail. Apart from this, the money transfer or the funds transfer between banks that involve high denominations must similarly be monitored through KYC norms and procedures.

How KYC Norms Help all Stakeholders

The reason why proper KYC norms can help is that if a particular customer or entity is in the red list or the black list being monitored, they can help spot and track transactions made by these entities. This means that proper identification of customers lead to better compliance and better monitoring. Further, KYC norms help banks and customers alike as the transactions carried out between the bank and the customers provide details of both so that any legal dispute arising out of such transactions can be resolved through documentation and data which would pinpoint the source of the dispute and help the arbitrators decide on who is guilty.

Concluding Thoughts

Finally, banks in recent times have embraced IT and systems to an extent that were not the case before and therefore, proper KYC norms complement and supplement the IT systems that the banks have and ensure compliance with the rules. In conclusion, it is clear more than ever that banks have to clean up their act and the regulators cannot overlook the transgressions anymore. This is the reason why well-maintained KYC norms help all stakeholders.

Difference between Corporate, Retail, Investment Banking, and Private Banking

The Difference between Retail, Corporate, and Investment Banking

Most of us when dealing with banks usually walk into the branch and get our work done we usually do not bother whether it is retail banking branch or a corporate banking branch. The difference between retail and corporate banking is that retail banking serves individuals and entities that are not corporates whereas corporate banking deals with large corporates who want to bank with that institution. The other end of the spectrum is the investment banking, which deals with high priced and low volumes deals like arranging for mergers and acquisitions, takeovers, and other deals aimed at the top notch of the management in the corporates. Further, it must be mentioned that whereas retail banking is volumes driven, corporate banking is a combination of volumes and size of the transactions, investment banking is purely driven by the size of the deals where volumes are usually low as the lack of it is made up by the fees earned by the investment bankers in individual deals. This means that the commissions on retail and corporate banking range from low to medium whereas for investment banking they range from high to very high.

The Components of the Retail, Corporate, and Investment Banking

Now that we have discussed the basic differences between the three arms of banks, we can now turn to the components of the three arms. Retail banking involves accepting deposits and giving loans to individuals and entities who are not corporates though in many countries, it is the practice to include organizations that resemble corporates in retail banking. The growth of corporate banking has been mainly driven by the need of the banks and the corporate sector to deal in foreign exchange transactions, to hedge their portfolios and in general, cater to the banking needs of the corporates that extend into other realms like deposits and loans of sizes that are very large. On the other hand, investment banking caters to the equity markets, the bond markets, the deals involving mergers, acquisitions, and the portfolio management as well. The point to be noted about the three arms of banking is that they comprise each customer segment that banks are supposed to cater to. As retail deals with individuals and organizations in some cases, corporate banking deals exclusively with the big corporates and investment banking deals with the mega deals that organizations do.

The Rise of Private Banking in Recent Years

In recent years, there has been a new area that banks are targeting and this is private banking or banking for the HNIs or the High Networth Individuals. This category of banking is purely directed towards individuals, entities, and trusts that have lot of money (indeed a fortune compared to retail consumers) which are then managed by the private bankers by assuring certain rates of return and rates of return above that that are determined by the performance of the portfolio. It needs to be mentioned that private banking sometimes encompasses all the other three arms as the presence of high Networth individuals and entities can include rich retail banking customers, corporates and trusts that need their wealth to be managed, and finally clients who are mega rich in the same way investment bankers transact mega deals.

How each arm of the Banks makes money ?

Apart from these differences, it must be mentioned that the other aspect about banking is that it follows the simple formula of determining the difference between the rate of interest it charges on its loans and the rate of interest that it pays to depositors. This is known as spread and the difference between the three arms of banking is that the spreads are different for each arm as well as the size of the transaction, which means that the multiplication of the spread and the size of the deal is the profit that the banks earn. This explains the difference in the various arms of the deals where low volumes are made up by the huge size of the deals in investment banking and the lesser sizes of the transactions are made up by the volumes in retail banking.

* 9 7 8 1 5 1 2 1 2 1 8 5 8 *